FESTIVECOOKING

THE BEST OF SINGAPORE'S RECIPES
MRS LEONG YEE SOO

mc Marshall Cavendish
Cuisine

FESTIVECOOKING THE BEST OF SINGAPORE'S RECIPES

All the recipes in this book are selected from the late Mrs Leong Yee Soo's original cookbooks, *Singaporean Cooking*, *Singaporean Cooking Vol 2*, *Celebration Cooking* and *The Best of Singapore Cooking*.

In *Singaporean Cooking* and *The Best of Singapore Cooking*, Mrs Rosa Lee, Mrs Dorothy Norris, Miss Marie Choo, Miss Patricia Lim, Mrs Dinah Sharif, Miss Iris Kng, Miss Chau Mei Po, Mrs Irene Oei and Miss Monica Funk were acknowledged for their help in making those books possible.

For this book the Publisher wishes to thank **Robinson & Co (S) Pte Ltd** for the loan of table and kitchen wares; **Mdm Hamidah Omar, Mdm Hatijah Mohd Hassan** and **Mdm Norah Mohd Hassan** for the loan of crockery, baking and cooking equipment.

Managing Editor	: Jamilah Mohd Hassan
Editor	: Sim Ee Waun
Art Direction/Designer	: Cynthia Ng, Jean Tan
Photographer	: Edmond Ho
Prop Stylists	: Yeo Puay Khoon, Illydea Seulasteri Ishak, Jean Tan
Food Preparation	: Gourmet Haven
Production Co-ordinator	: Nor Sidah Haron

Food pictures on pages 25, 61 and 141, and utensil pictures on pages 158, 160 and 162 by Sam Yeo.

© 2005 Marshall Cavendish International (Asia) Private Limited

Published by Marshall Cavendish Cuisine
An imprint of Marshall Cavendish International (Asia) Private Limited
A member of Times Publishing Limited
Times Centre, 1 New Industrial Road, Singapore 536196
Tel: (65) 6213 9300   Fax: (65) 6285 4871   E-mail: te@sg.marshallcavendish.com
Online Bookstore: www.marshallcavendish.com/genref

Malaysian Office:
Marshall Cavendish (Malaysia) Sdn Bhd (3024-D)
(General & Reference Publishing)
(Formerly known as Federal Publications Sdn Berhad)
Times Subang
Lot 46, Persiaran Teknologi Subang
Subang Hi-Tech Industrial Park
Batu Tiga, 40000 Shah Alam
Selangor Darul Ehsan, Malaysia
Tel: (603) 5635 2191, 5628 6888   Fax: (603) 5635 2706   E-mail: cchong@my.marshallcavendish.com

National Library Board Singapore Cataloguing in Publication Data
Leong, Yee Soo.
Festive cooking / Leong Yee Soo. – Singapore :- Marshall Cavendish Cuisine,- c2005.
p. cm. – (The best of Singapore's recipes)
Includes index.
ISBN : 981-232-651-0

1. Holiday cookery- – Singapore. 2. Cookery, Singapore. I. Title.
II. Series: The best of Singapore's recipes

TX739
641.568 — dc21   SLS2004142759

Printed in Singapore by Utopia Press Pte Ltd

CONTENTS ● ● ● ● ●

CONTENTS

PREFACE

MY GRANDMOTHER loved to cook and she loved to cook for the family. I remember as a child licking the cake mix from the bowl and waiting anxiously for the cake to come out of the oven. Our family had the benefit of her wonderful cooking and instructions on food preparation and methodology first hand. As in the past, my grandmother would always refer to her cookbooks while cooking, and today, many of our family members still continue with the same practice.

She spent more than 20 years perfecting her skills, constantly trying to improve her skills by experimenting with new kitchen equipment, technology and recipes. She had created her own recipes to be an easy and reliable guide so that even busy working adults could prepare delicious home cooked food. Her cookbooks were very much written to serve the needs of busy families and preserve the tradition of family cooking, especially with the increasingly hectic lifestyle of Singaporeans.

In this book, the recipes have now been reproduced with a new arrangement and photographs. It continues in the same tradition of the earlier books and pays attention to the careful preparation of dishes and a good choice of ingredients. In addition, all the useful cooking tips are still included.

We hope this book gives you a chance to experience good home cooking and good memories together with family and friends, cooking and eating together.

This book is dedicated to our grandmother's memory as a great cook, a progressive woman in her field, beloved mother, grandmother and great grandmother.

LEONG PAT LYNN & LEONG SUE LYNN

CANDLENUTS

If unavailable, use almonds, cashew nuts, Brazil nuts or macadamia nuts.

COCONUT

The milk from the coconut you use plays a very important part in the type of food or cakes that you are preparing. Be very careful and selective when choosing a coconut. Coconuts do not come in one standard size, age and richness.

- The skinned, grated coconut referred to throughout the book is coconut which has the brown skin removed. This is to give the milk an extra whiteness. It also gives a rich natural colour to the food.
- When buying a coconut, bear in mind the type of food or cake you are preparing. For most types of food that require coconut milk, choose a freshly cut coconut with a dark brown skin as this gives rich and sweet milk. For cakes, you need to see to the requirements of your recipe. For example, if the recipe calls for 'coarsely grated coconut', then you should choose one that has a light brown skin; it is younger than the dark brown and is tender and not stringy. For special recipes like 'Sar-Sargon', you require coconut that is tender and young, ie. the skin of the coconut must be pale in colour.
- For cakes that need coarsely grated coconut to be sprinkled over, it is safer to rub a little fine salt lightly over the coconut. Place it in a shallow baking tin and steam over rapidly boiling water for 3 minutes. Cool completely before use. This will keep the coconut from turning sour.
- For every 455 g (1 lb) of grated coconut, you should be able to extract about 225–255 ml (1–1$\frac{1}{8}$ cups) milk when the coconut is fresh. Therefore, make sure the coconut is freshly cut for the day and not one that has been cut and kept overnight. See that the coconut is free of mildew or has not turned yellow in some parts.

- One interesting point to note is that the amount of milk you get from a kilogramme of grated coconut depends on the machine that grates the coconut. The rollers used in the grating machines at coconut stalls come in different degrees of fineness. As such, a machine using fine tooth rollers gives you more milk than one with coarse tooth rollers.
- To squeeze coconut for No.1 milk: take a piece of white muslin 30-cm (12-in) square, put in a small fistful, or about 55 g (2 oz), of coconut and squeeze and twist at the same time. For No.2 milk, add the amount of water required and squeeze hard.

Freezing Coconut Milk
- Buy 1.4–1.8 kg (3–4 lb) of grated coconut, squeeze for No.1 milk and set aside. Add 170 ml ($\frac{3}{4}$ cup) water to each 455 g (1 lb) of coconut and squeeze for No.2 milk. Collect separately. Pour the No.1 and No.2 milk in separate ice-cube trays. When frozen, remove from ice-tray and pack into plastic bags and store in the freezer. It is very useful to have a stock of frozen coconut milk always in case you need it at any time of the day. It can be used to make curries and all types of cakes.
- To use frozen coconut milk, chop the amount required. Place a little water in a saucepan and bring to a boil. Place the frozen coconut milk in a small enamel basin, place basin over the water and allow the frozen coconut to thaw, stirring occasionally. Remove coconut milk to cool as soon as it turns liquid.

KITCHEN WISDOM & TIPS ON TECHNIQUES

Making Coconut Oil for Nyonya Cakes

In a saucepan, combine 115 g (4 oz) grated coconut, 225 ml (1 cup) corn oil and 8 screwpine (*pandan*) leaves that have been cut into pieces. Bring to a boil and cook until coconut turns dark brown. Pour oil through a metal sieve and cool before use. Store in refrigerator to preserve freshness and for future use.

COOKING MEAT

Pork chops should be cooked over moderate heat in a very hot pan or grilled under a hot grill. This will seal in the meat juices. Brown on both sides, turning over twice; then turn the heat down to medium and cook until done, about 15–20 minutes.

For bacon, cut off the rind and snip the fat in two or three places to prevent bacon from curling during frying.

Fillet steak is the best and most tender of meat cuts; next comes sirloin, scotch, porterhouse, rump and minute steak. Marinating a steak before cooking not only gives it a better flavour but also helps to make it tender. Minute steak, however, is best grilled or fried without marinating.

COOKING OIL AND FATS

To get the best results, particularly when cooking Chinese dishes, use an equal portion of both lard and cooking oil. It gives the dish a special fragrance. In recipes that specify that lard is preferable to cooking oil, use lard in order to get its distinct flavour.

For deep-frying, always use either refined deodorised coconut oil, palm cooking oil or corn oil. Do not use olive oil.

COOKING VEGETABLES

To fry leafy vegetables, separate the leaves from the stalk. The stalks should be placed in the pan together with any other ingredients and cooked first. Stir-fry for a minute or so before adding the leaves.

To blanch vegetables, bring a saucepan of water to the boil over very high heat. When the water is boiling, add some salt, sugar and a tablespoonful of cooking oil. Add the stalks, cook for $1/2$ minute and then add the leaves. Cook for another $1/2$ minute. Use a wire ladle to remove the vegetables and drain in a colander. Rinse under a running tap and drain well before use.

Vegetables like long beans and cabbage should be cooked for 5–7 minutes only, to retain their sweetness and crispness.

When boiling bean sprouts, it is important to place them in boiling water for 1 minute. Do not add any cooking oil. Remove and drain with a wire ladle. Transfer to a basin of cold water and soak for 10 minutes or until cold. Spread thinly in a colander until ready for use. The bean sprouts will then keep without 'souring'.

FRYING

1. Before frying, ensure that the the pan is very hot before you pour in the cooking oil. To get the best results when frying vegetables:
   - Use an iron wok (*kuali*) as it can take and retain extreme heat, which is most important.
   - Add the cooking oil to a smoking hot wok. This prevents food from sticking to the bottom. But do not allow the oil to become smoking hot as overheated fat or oil turns bitter and loses its fine flavour.
2. For deep-frying, the cooking oil must be smoky, that is, when a faint haze of smoke rises from the oil. It is then ready for frying.
   - When deep-frying in large quantities, put enough food in the pan and keep the oil boiling all the time.

- Make sure the fat is heated until smoking hot each time you put in food to be fried.
- When frying large pieces of meat or a whole chicken, the heat must be very high for the first 5 minutes to seal in the juices. After that, lower the heat for the rest of the cooking time. This gives the meat or chicken a nice golden colour and allows it to be cooked right through.

3. After frying food that is coated with flour or breadcrumbs (this also seals in the meat juices), filter the oil through a wire sieve lined thinly with cotton wool. The oil will come out clean and free from sediments.
    - Add more fresh oil to the strained oil for future use.
4. Cooking oil that has been used to deep-fry fish and prawns should be kept separate for future use and kept for cooking fish and prawns only.
5. You may clarify hot oil by squeezing some lemon juice into it, but remember to turn off the heat first. Strain and store for future use.
6. Butter will not take intense heat when frying, so put in some cooking oil before the butter.
7. Dust food with seasoned flour before coating with or dipping in batter for frying.

KAFFIR LIME LEAVES
Locally called *daun limau purut*, it has waxy dark green, double leaves with a distinct fragrance. To slice finely, roll it up tightly and slice thinly parallel to the central vein. Discard the central vein which will come out in one complete strip after slicing.

LARD
The oil extracted from pork fat after it has been fried is called lard. Dice the pork fat before frying. Do not overcook or burn the fat, otherwise the oil extracted will be dark and bitter. Unlike butter or margarine, lard can take intense heat without burning so it is most suitable for food that has to be cooked over high heat.

LEMON GRASS
Lemon grass gives a pleasant fragrance to cooked dishes. Use lemon rind as a substitute only when this is not available. The fragrance comes from the bottom 7 cm (3 in) of the stalk nearest the root end. The green outer layer is removed before use. To bruise or crush lemon grass, bash with the flat surface of a cleaver or chopper.

LIME PASTE
The lime paste mentioned in some of the recipes refers to the white chalky edible lime that is used for betelnut chewing. It can be bought at any Indian grocery.

Chillies retain their crispness in certain recipes when they are soaked in lime water.

SEASONING
The salt used in many of these recipes is local fine salt and not the fine table salt. Fine table salt is used mostly in Western cakes where it can be sifted together with the flour. As table salt is finer, it is more salty than the local fine salt. So measure less salt if you use fine table salt.

Use your discretion when seasoning with salt, sugar, chilli or tamarind pulp (*asam*). Season to your own taste as there is no hard and fast rule for seasoning food. However, one must be precise and follow the recipe to get the best results.

MSG in recipes refers to monosodium glutamate. As a substitute, chicken stock may be used. Use 1 chicken cube for 1 tsp MSG.

KITCHEN WISDOM & TIPS ON TECHNIQUES

SCREWPINE LEAVES
Commonly called *pandan* leaves, this local plant is a rich emerald green and has long, smooth pointed leaves. It imparts a special fragrance and is used widely in Asian desserts and kuih. There is no substitute. Before tying it into a knot, tear each leaf lengthwise to release the fragrance.

SELECTING MEAT, POULTRY AND SEAFOOD
Pork
Should be pink, the fat very white and the skin thin.

Beef
Choose meat that is light red and the cross-grain smooth and fine. The same applies to mutton. Do not buy dark coloured meat with fat that is yellow.

Chicken
Fresh local chickens have a much better taste and flavour than frozen ones. Frozen chicken is more suitable for roasting, frying or grilling. When buying local chicken, select one with white, smooth skin. The tip of the breastbone should be soft and pliable when pressed with the thumb. When selecting chicken for steaming, choose one that is young and tender and weighs about 1 kg (approximately $2^1/_2$ lb). For Hainanese chicken rice, choose one that is plump at the breasts and thighs and weighs 1.6–1.8 kg (approximately $3^1/_2$–4 lb). For grilled chicken or roast spring chicken, choose a 680–795 g ($1^1/_2$–$1^3/_4$ lb) chicken. A 1.5 kg (3–$3^1/_2$ lb) chicken is best for curries and other spicy dishes.

Duck
Select as for chicken. The smaller ones are mostly used for soups and the larger ducks for roasting or braising.

Fish
When buying fish, first of all make sure that the flesh is firm to the touch. The eyes should be shiny, the gills blood-red and the scales silvery white. Squeezing lemon juice over fish will whiten it and keep it firm when boiling or steaming.

Mix tamarind, salt and some sugar to marinate fish for $1/_2$ hour before cooking curries or tamarind dishes.

Prawns
Fresh prawns have shiny shells and are firm to the touch. The head is firmly attached to the body. Avoid buying prawns with heads loosely hanging on.

Cuttlefish
When cuttlefish is very fresh, the body is well rounded, firm and shiny. The head is stuck fast to the body and the ink pouch in the stomach is firmly attached.

SUBSTITUTE INGREDIENTS
- The purplish variety of onion is a good substitute for shallots.
- If fresh ginger, lemon grass and galangal are not easily available, use the powdered forms.
- It is always advisable to use powdered turmeric.
- Almonds, cashew nuts, Brazil nuts or macadamia nuts can be used if candlenuts are not available.

THICKENING
For Chinese dishes, thickening means to thicken the gravy so as to coat the food rather than have the gravy running over the serving plate. Cornflour is a common thickening agent and refers here to tapioca flour sold in the local markets. It is also known as sago flour (refined quality, and not the type used to starch clothes).

ALUMINIUM FRYING PANS

Suitable for deep-frying as they retain a steady heat and give food a nice golden brown colour. Frying chilli paste in an aluminium pan will give the mixture a natural bright colour whereas an iron wok (*kuali*) will result in a darker paste, possibly with a slight taste of iron.

ALUMINIUM SAUCEPAN

The heavy flat-bottomed pan is the best buy. It is suitable for the electric or gas stove. Food is cooked easily without burning. A thin saucepan will buckle when it is overheated and will not be in contact with the electric hot plate.

CHINA CLAYPOT

Chicken and pork are usually braised and stewed in the China claypot. It simmers food very nicely without burning and has a lower rate of evaporation than other saucepans. It also retains the special flavour of foods and is widely used in Chinese homes. It is also used to cook rice and porridge. Buy one with a smooth, glazed finish.

COPPER PANS

Copper pans are rarely used for Asian recipes. A copper pan has its own rare qualities. Salted mustard has a very bright green colour when boiled in a copper pan. Copper pans are very rarely used, however, as they are very expensive.

ENAMEL SAUCEPANS

Enamel saucepans are more suitable for soups and certain types of food that contain acid like tamarind or vinegar. Chipped enamelware is vulnerable to rust.

IRON WOK

Most Chinese prefer the iron wok (*kuali*) to the aluminium one chiefly because the iron wok can retain extreme heat before the other ingredients are added. In an iron wok, food cooks in a shorter period of time and retain its flavour and crispness. The most important point to remember is that fried food and pounded ingredients will not stick to the bottom of the wok when it is well heated.

To season an iron wok

Place some grated coconut and water to fill up three-quarters of the wok, and boil until dry. Stir occasionally until the coconut turns black, approximately 3–4 hours.

Daily care: Do not use any detergent. Wipe wok well after each wash. If it is to be stored for a long period, grease wok lightly to prevent rust.

NON-STICK PANS

There are many brands of non-stick pans to select from. Choose carefully. Whenever possible, buy the best quality products as they work out to be the most cost effective in the long run.

Some points to remember when using non-stick pans

- Non-stick pans are ideal for frying fish and soft bean curd. In a non-stick pan, food that is to be braised or simmered require less liquid. Food does not burn easily in a non-stick pan nor does the gravy evaporate as quickly as in an ordinary pan.
- The Teflon in a non-stick pan should not be heated through. If this happens, the pan may lose its non-stick qualities. Since stir-frying requires high heat, do not stir-fry in a non-stick pan. It is always best to stir-fry in an iron wok.
- Do not use the non-stick pan as a steamer as it will again damage the Teflon.
- Never use a metal slice on a non-stick pan.
- Always pour in the cooking oil or gravy first before putting on the heat.

KITCHEN EQUIPMENT

PESTLE AND MORTAR
Insist on local granite which is white with black/grey spots. To season the pounder, grind a small handful of fine sea sand in the mortar until both the pestle and mortar are reasonably smooth.

STAINLESS STEEL PANS
Stainless steel pans look attractive and are easily cleaned, but do not heat evenly. Food burns easily, too.

SUPPLEMENTARY RECIPES

Crisp-fried Shallots
Many recipes call for crisp-fried shallots to be used as a flavourful garnish.

- Peel and slice shallots thinly and dip in salt water for a while. Rinse and drain well.
- Scatter sliced shallots on absorbent paper to dry or roll up in a tea towel for $1/2$ hour. Heat enough cooking oil for deep-frying until smoking hot. Add the sliced shallots and stir-fry over high heat until shallots turn light brown.
- Reduce the heat and continue stirring until the shallots are light golden brown. Remove at once with a wire sieve to drain. Scatter on absorbent paper to cool.
- Store in a clean, dry bottle immediately. The shallots keep crisp for months in an airtight bottle.

Fried Pounded Garlic
- Peel and pound garlic or use blender to mince the garlic.
- Place garlic in a wire sieve and immerse in salt water. Drain. Use a thin piece of muslin to further squeeze out the water.
- In a heated wok, add enough cooking oil for deep-frying. When the oil is smoking hot, put the garlic and stir-fry until it turns light brown. Reduce the heat to very low and continue stirring until garlic becomes a light golden brown.
- Remove at once with a wire sieve and scatter on absorbent paper. Cool and store as for crisp-fried shallots.

Note:
The crisp-fried shallots and garlic do not retain much oil when the heat is turned up just before removing from wok.

Rice

- Wash rice until water runs clear.
- Use 55 ml ($^1/_4$ cup) of water for every 30 g (1 oz) of rice.
- For 455 g (1 lb) of rice, use between 800–910 ml ($3^1/_2$–4 cups) water, depending on the quality of the rice.
- Boil the rice until the water evaporates, leaving steam holes when dry. Reduce heat to low and cook for a further $^1/_2$ hour. About 455 g (1 lb) of rice is sufficient for 8 servings.

Dried Chilli Paste

Dried chillies	225 g (8 oz), stems removed
Water	450 ml (2 cups)

- Place chillies in a saucepan three-quarter filled with cold water.
- Bring to a boil and cook for 5 minutes. Cover pan and leave chillies to soak for 10 minutes. Drain.
- Place chillies in a large basin and wash until water runs clear. Drain.
- Using an electric blender, blend half of the chillies with 225 ml (1 cup) water until very fine. Remove paste and repeat process with the other half of the chillies and water.
- Store chilli paste in a plastic container. Keep in freezer until needed.

Note:
Keep chilli paste rotating while blending. Add a little water if paste is stuck.

Wet Rice or Glutinous Rice Flour

Fine rice or glutinous rice flour	625 g (1 lb 6 oz)
Cold water	425 ml ($1^3/_4$ cups and 2 Tbsp)

- Place flour in a mixing bowl and gradually pour in the cold water. Stir until it becomes a firm paste.
- Use the amount required for each recipe and keep the remainder in the freezer for future use.

Note:
- The paste will keep in the freezer for 1–2 months if stored in plastic bags flattened to 2.5 cm (1 inch) thick slabs.
- Recommended brands: Superior Quality Thai Rice and Glutinous Rice Flour (Erawan Brand); Fine Rice Flour (Seagull trademark); freshly ground wet rice or glutinous rice flour are available at local wet markets.

Alkaline Water

White alkaline crystal	625 g (1 lb 6 oz)
Hot water	680 ml (3 cups)

- Place alkaline crystal in a porcelain jar or bowl. Add the hot water and stir with a wooden spoon to dissolve the crystals. Let it stand overnight.
- Strain alkaline water through a fine muslin. Store the alkaline water in a bottle for future use.

Note:
- Prepared alkaline water can be kept for almost a year. Store in a bottle.
- Alkaline water is now available at specialty bakery suppliers such as Phoon Huat.

partynibbles

FESTIVE COOKING – THE BEST OF SINGAPORE'S RECIPES

Peanuts and Anchovy Crunch

INGREDIENTS

Dried chillies	55 g (2 oz), soaked in hot water for 10 minutes
Shallots	170 g (6 oz), peeled
Garlic	6 cloves, peeled
Shrimp paste (*belacan*)	1 Tbsp
Cooking oil	225 ml (1 cup)
Dried anchovies (*ikan bilis*)	285 g (10 oz), washed and drained
Roasted peanuts	285 g (10 oz), skinned
Sugar	2–3 Tbsp

METHOD

- Place chillies in a pestle and mortar and pound. Add shallots, garlic and shrimp paste and continue pounding until very fine. Set aside.
- Heat cooking oil until smoking hot. Fry anchovies in batches until crispy. Drain. (Heat the oil each time before frying the anchovies.)
- When all the anchovies have been fried, strain the oil into a container for use again later.
- In a clean pan, place half of the strained oil and heat. Fry the pounded chilli and garlic mixture over moderate heat until fragrant and light brown. Add the anchovies, roasted peanuts and sugar and stir for 2 minutes.
- Transfer to a large plate to cool. Store in an airtight bottle.

Note:
The oil for frying anchovies must be very hot. Fry anchovies for 1–2 minutes, reduce heat and let the fish brown and crisp right through. Another way to serve crispy anchovies is to cook them in *sambal*. (See recipe below.)

Sambal for Crispy Anchovies

INGREDIENTS

Dried chillies	115 g (4 oz), washed
Garlic	1 clove, peeled
Shallots or onions	115 g (4 oz), peeled
Shrimp paste (*belacan*)	55 g (2 oz)
Coconut	170 g (6 oz), grated
Water	225 ml (1 cup)
Cooking oil	170 ml (³/₄ cup)

Seasoning

Sugar	4 level Tbsp
Salt	¹/₄ tsp
MSG	1 tsp, optional
Tamarind pulp (*asam*)	1 Tbsp, mixed with 4 Tbsp water, squeezed and strained

METHOD

- Soak dried chillies in water to soften. When soft, combine chillies with garlic, shallots or onions and shrimp paste and pound to a fine paste. Set aside.
- Place grated coconut and water in a bowl. Using a piece of muslin, squeeze coconut to extract No.2 coconut milk. Set aside.
- Place some cooking oil in a heated wok and heat through. Add chilli paste and one-third of the milk and fry over moderate heat until fragrant.
- Stir in seasoning ingredients and the remaining coconut milk. Lower heat and simmer for 2 minutes.
- Transfer to a bowl to cool. Divide into four portions, pack in plastic bags and freeze for future use.

Note:
Each portion of the *sambal* can be mixed with 680 g (1¹/₂ lb) of crispy anchovies and served as a side dish for *nasi lemak*.

Fried Coconut Floss

INGREDIENTS

Shallots	55 g (2 oz), peeled
Shrimp paste (*belacan*)	1 tsp
Candlenuts	3
Red chilli	1, small, seeded
Coconut	455 g (1 lb), coarsely grated
Salt	1 tsp
Sugar	1 tsp

METHOD

- In a mortar and pestle, pound shallots, shrimp paste, candlenuts and chilli to a paste.
- Mix paste with grated coconut, salt and sugar. Fry in a heated wok over moderate heat for 10 minutes. Reduce heat and continue to fry until coconut is dry. Stir often to prevent burning.
- Cool and store in a clean, dry bottle.

Note:
Coconut should be dry, grainy and golden in colour.

Crispy Pork Floss

INGREDIENTS

Pork	1.4 kg (3 lb), lean, a whole chunk
Water	455 ml (2 cups)
Castor sugar	170 g (6 oz)

Seasoning

Soy sauce	5 Tbsp
Dark soy sauce	1¹/₂ Tbsp
Pepper	1¹/₂ tsp
Salt	1 tsp
MSG	2 tsp, optional

METHOD

- Cook pork in a pressure cooker with water for 1–1¹/₂ hours.
- Add seasoning ingredients and boil over moderate heat until almost dry.
- Remove meat, shred very finely, add the stock (ie. liquid in which the pork has been cooked) and mix well.
- In a heated wok, fry the shredded pork until almost dry. Reduce heat, sprinkle with sugar while pork is still moist and stir fry until dry and crispy.
- Set aside to cool, then store in an airtight container.

Note:
Pound the pork with a mallet before shredding it.

Otak–otak Putih

BAKED FISH PARCELS WITH RICH COCONUT CREAM

INGREDIENTS

Water	4 Tbsp
Coconut	225 g (8 oz), skinned and grated
Fish meat	570 g (1 1/4 lb)
Egg white	2, lightly beaten
Banana leaves	40 pieces, 20–25 cm (8–10 in)

Seasoning

Salt	1/2 Tbsp
MSG	1 1/2 tsp, optional
Sugar	1 tsp
Tapioca flour	1 tsp
Pepper	A dash
Galangal juice	1 tsp

METHOD

- In a bowl, combine water and grated coconut. Using a piece of muslin, squeeze to extract milk.
- Stir the seasoning ingredients into the coconut milk and set aside.
- Put fish meat into a food processor and blend into a fine paste. With the motor running, gradually add in the coconut milk and continue blending until well combined.
- Transfer the fish paste into a large bowl and add in the egg whites. Beat until stiff.
- Place a banana leaf on the table. Wet your hands and place some fish paste onto the leaf. Fold the longer ends of the leaf over the paste to cover, and seal the open ends with toothpicks. Repeat with the remaining paste and leaves.
- Place the fish parcels in a pan and fry until cooked, or place under a hot grill for 7–8 minutes. Serve.

Note:
To get a finer texture for this dish, use wolf herring (*ikan parang*) or a combination of Spanish Mackerel (*ikan tenggiri*) and *ikan keledek* in equal portions. Beat until stiff.

reuniondinner

FESTIVE COOKING – THE BEST OF SINGAPORE'S RECIPES

Chicken, Prawn and Jellyfish Salad

INGREDIENTS

Australian lettuce	115 g (4 oz), shredded
Steamed chicken	170 g (6 oz), breast meat, shredded
Jellyfish	225 g (8 oz), shredded, processed and seasoned (*see recipe below*)
Prawns	10, shelled, halved lengthwise, deveined and boiled
Coleslaw dressing	4 tsp
Sesame seeds	2 tsp, toasted

METHOD

- Heap shredded lettuce on a large serving plate.
- Place chicken on the lettuce. Spread the jellyfish on top of the chicken and arrange the prawns over it. Chill.
- When ready to serve, pour coleslaw dressing over the salad and sprinkle with sesame seeds.

To treat and season jellyfish

INGREDIENTS

Alkaline water	6 Tbsp (*recipe on page 13*)
Cold water	1.7 litres (6³/₄ cups)
Salted jellyfish	600 g (1 lb 5 oz)

Seasoning for 225 g (8 oz) jellyfish

Soy sauce	3 tsp
Sugar	1 tsp
MSG	1¹/₂ tsp, optional
Peanut or corn oil	2 tsp
Sesame oil	1 tsp

METHOD

- Combine alkaline water and cold water in a non-reactive container and soak the jellyfish for 48 hours or until jellyfish swells and softens.
- Wash in cold water and cut each into 2 or 4 pieces.
- Bring a saucepan of water to a rapid boil. Blanch jellyfish, then plunge it into a basin of cold water. (Bring water back to a fast boil each time you blanch the jellyfish.)
- Drain jellyfish and weigh out 225 g (8 oz). Roll jellyfish in tea towels until dry and shred thinly. Mix in the seasoning.
- Keep the rest of the jellyfish in a container of water and store in the refrigerator for future use.

Note:
Prepared jellyfish can be stored in the refrigerator for at least 2–3 weeks if the water is changed every 4th day. Blanch in hot water and roll in dry tea towel to dry before use.

Shredded Duck and Fruit Salad

INGREDIENTS

Lettuce	1 cup, shredded
Processed jellyfish	1 cup, shredded
Cucumber	1 cup, shredded
Honeydew melon	1 cup, cut into thin strips
Roast duck	1 cup, shredded

Garnish

Walnuts	1/2 cup, chopped
Peanuts	1/2 cup, ground and roasted
Sesame seeds	3 Tbsp, toasted

METHOD

- Place shredded ingredients and honeydew melon strips on a large serving plate, starting with the lettuce at the bottom and layering according to the ingredients listed, with the roast duck on top. Chill.
- Before serving, sprinkle over with walnuts, peanuts and sesame seeds. Pour dressing (*see recipe below*) over and serve.

Roast Duck Salad Dressing

INGREDIENTS

Sour plum sauce (*sung boey choew*)	4 Tbsp
Apricot jam	4 Tbsp
Sweet chilli sauce	1 Tbsp
Vinegar	1 tsp
Peanut oil	1 Tbsp
Ginger wine	1 tsp, optional
Sugar	1 tsp
Sesame oil	1/2 tsp

METHOD

- Combine all the ingredients in a small saucepan and stir over low heat until heated through and blended.
- Strain mixture, heat through again and serve with the salad.

Shredded Jellyfish

INGREDIENTS

Processed jellyfish	455 g (1 lb)
Lettuce	1, shredded
Sesame seeds	2 Tbsp

Dressing

Soy sauce	2 tsp
Sugar	$^1/_2$ tsp
MSG	1 tsp, optional
Sesame oil	1 tsp

METHOD

- Combine dressing ingredients in a bowl and stir to blend. Set aside.
- Bring a saucepan of water to a rolling boil. Blanch jellyfish (in a single piece or cut into 2 or 3 pieces) for about 10 seconds, then plunge it into a basin of cold water immediately. Drain and wrap in a large kitchen towel to absorb the water.
- When ready to serve, cut jellyfish into thin strips with a sharp knife.
- Place jellyfish in a bowl and toss with the dressing.
- Place on a serving plate lined with shredded green lettuce and sprinkle over with sesame seeds. Serve.

Note:
If you are using salted jellyfish, prepare it by first washing away the excess salt. Then immerse it completely in a bowl of water with 1 Tbsp lye water. Soak overnight to let it swell. The soaked jellyfish should be a little spongy and not leathery to the touch. Allow the jellyfish to soak in fresh cold water for 10 minutes before using in this recipe.

Seven-treasure Steamed Duck

INGREDIENTS

Duck	1.4 kg (3 lb), cleaned
Pork	455 g (1 lb), coarsely minced
Chinese mushrooms	55 g (2 oz)
Pearl barley	85 g (3 oz)
Lard or cooking oil	2 Tbsp
Garlic	1 tsp, chopped
Ginger	6 thick slices
Ham	55 g (2 oz), diced
Gingko nuts	115 g (4 oz), canned
Lotus seeds	115 g (4 oz), canned
Duck livers	2, boiled and diced
Duck gizzards	2, boiled and diced

Duck Marinade

Ginger juice	1 tsp
Salt	1 tsp
Sugar	1 tsp
MSG	1 tsp, optional
Brandy	1 tsp
Soy sauce	1 Tbsp

Pork Marinade

Salt	1 tsp
Sugar	1 tsp
MSG	1 tsp, optional
Fish sauce	2 Tbsp

Seasoning

Salt	1 tsp
Sugar	2 tsp
MSG	1 tsp, optional
Chicken stock cube	1
Dark soy sauce	1 Tbsp
Thai fish sauce	2 Tbsp
Pepper	$1/2$ tsp

Thickening

Tapioca flour	1 Tbsp
Water	5 Tbsp

METHOD

- Boil duck in a large saucepan of water with 1 Tbsp salt for 5 minutes. Drain and pat dry.
- Marinate the duck and pork separately with their respective marinades. Set aside.
- Soak mushrooms in 225 ml (1 cup) hot water to soften. When soft, dice mushrooms and set aside. Reserve the mushroom water as well for use later.
- Place pearl barley in a pan with 285 ml ($1^1/4$ cups) water and bring to a gentle boil for $1/2$ hour. Set aside.
- Place the 2 Tbsp lard or cooking oil in a pan and heat. Add garlic and 2 slices of ginger and fry until light brown. Add mushrooms and stir.
- Increase heat to high. Add the ham and marinated pork and cook until pork changes colour. Add seasoning ingredients, gingko nuts, lotus seeds, barley, diced liver and gizzard, 340 ml ($1^1/2$ cups) water and reserved mushroom water. Cook over high heat for 5 minutes. Turn down the heat, then let it simmer for another 10 minutes.
- Transfer to a dish to cool.
- When cool, stuff duck with the meat mixture. Use a sharp skewer to close the cavity.
- Place the duck on a large dish. Place the extra filling, including the liquid, beside the duck. Top with the 4 slices of ginger.
- Steam the duck for $2^1/2$–3 hours until tender.
- Combine thickening ingredients. When duck is ready, stir in the thickening gradually until it is blended into the gravy.
- Transfer to a serving plate and serve at once.

Note:
Replenish water in the steamer when necessary.

Excess oil should be removed from the gravy before serving.

Deep-fried Spicy Boneless Chicken

INGREDIENTS

Chicken thighs	6
Cooking oil for deep-frying	
Lettuce	
Cucumber	1, skinned and thickly sliced
Tomatoes	2, sliced
Sesame oil	1 Tbsp
Spring onions	2, cut into 1-cm (1/2-in) lengths

Marinade

Ginger juice	1 tsp
Soy sauce	4 tsp
Dark soy sauce	1 Tbsp
Chinese wine or sherry	1 Tbsp
Spring onions	2, bruised
Five-spice powder	1/2 tsp
Sugar	1 tsp sugar
MSG	1/2 tsp, optional

METHOD

- Wash and debone chicken thighs. Wipe dry, rub with marinade and leave for 1 hour. When marinated, discard spring onions and set aside the remaining or excess marinade.
- Heat cooking oil in a wok until very hot. Deep-fry chicken pieces over high heat for 2 minutes. Reduce heat to moderate and cook until light brown on both sides. Drain and set aside to cool for 10 minutes.
- Reheat oil in a clean wok. When hot, return the chicken to the wok and fry for 1/2 minute over high heat. Remove with a metal sieve and drain oil. Set chicken aside to cool for 5 minutes.
- Slice chicken into 2.5-cm (1-in) pieces and arrange on a bed of lettuce. Garnish with cucumber and tomato slices.
- Pour oil from the pan leaving behind 2 Tbsp. Add sesame oil and the leftover marinade, and bring to the boil. Add the spring onions, stir to heat through then pour over chicken. Serve.

Steamed Chicken and Abalone

INGREDIENTS

Chicken	1.2 kg (2 lb 11 oz)
Salt	1 tsp
Garlic	6 cloves, peeled and lightly crushed
Spring onions	4, knotted
Ginger	55 g (2 oz), peeled and lightly crushed
Boiling water	3 Tbsp
Lettuce for garnishing	
Abalone	1 can, about 455 g (1 lb), sliced (set aside liquid)
Cornflour	1 Tbsp, mixed with 2 Tbsp water
Lard	1 Tbsp
Tomato for garnishing	

Dressing

Abalone liquid	115 ml (1/2 cup) (from above)
Salt	1/4 tsp
MSG	1/2 tsp, optional
Sugar	1/2 tsp
Sesame oil	1 tsp
Sherry	1 tsp

METHOD

- Rub the chicken all over with 1 tsp salt.
- Place garlic, spring onions and ginger in the cavity of the chicken and set aside for 1/2 hour.
- Place the chicken on a plate and pour the boiling water over the chicken. Steam for 30–45 minutes until cooked.
- When the chicken is cool enough to handle, cut it into pieces and set aside. Reserve the stock or remaining liquid for use later.
- Place lettuce on a large serving plate, arrange the sliced abalone on top and then the chicken.
- Prepare the dressing: In a saucepan, combine 115 ml (1/2 cup) of the abalone liquid, the reserved chicken stock and the dressing ingredients. Bring to the boil and stir in the cornflour solution. When it comes back to the boil, stir in the lard. Pour dressing over the chicken and garnish with sliced tomato. Serve at once.

Yim Kok Kai

CHICKEN COOKED IN SALT

INGREDIENTS

Young chicken	1, whole, about 900 g (2 lb)
Salt	1 1/2 tsp
MSG	1 tsp, optional
Five-spice powder	1/4 tsp
Sherry	1 tsp
Cooking oil	1 tsp
Coarse salt	3.6 kg (8 lb)

METHOD

- Clean and wash chicken thoroughly. Remove the neck and feet, and wipe dry.
- Rub 1/2 tsp salt, MSG, if using, and five-spice powder on the inside of chicken. Rub 1 tsp salt, sherry and cooking oil over the surface of chicken and set aside to marinate for 1 hour.
- Wrap chicken up in 2 large pieces of greaseproof paper.
- Line a shallow baking tin with aluminium foil, fill with coarse salt and heat it in a very hot oven until very hot. (Alternatively, you can fry the coarse salt in an old wok.)
- Pour half the heated salt into a large Chinese clay pot and place the chicken in the middle of the pot. Pour the rest of the salt over the chicken and cover.
- Place the claypot over low heat on the stove and cook for 1 hour until the chicken is cooked. Serve hot.

Note:
As the salt has to be very hot, it cannot be heated in a claypot as the pot may crack. If you do not have a claypot, use a heavy aluminium saucepan large enough to hold the chicken and all the salt. Cover with a tight fitting lid.

Paper–wrapped Chicken

INGREDIENTS

Chicken	1.4 kg (3 lb), cut into pieces
Cooking oil for deep-frying	
Greaseproof paper	

Marinade

Cornflour	1 Tbsp
Water	2 Tbsp
Salt	1 tsp
MSG	1 tsp, optional
Sugar	1 tsp
Sesame oil	2 tsp
Pepper	1 tsp
Soy sauce	1 Tbsp
Ginger juice	1 Tbsp
Lard or cooking oil	3 Tbsp
Brandy or sherry	1 Tbsp

METHOD

- Cut the greaseproof paper into 20-cm (8-in) squares.
- Combine marinade ingredients in a bowl and rub over the chicken. Set aside for 2 hours.
- Place a few pieces of chicken in each piece of greaseproof paper and staple the edges to form a sealed packet.
- Deep-fry the chicken, a few packets at a time, until light brown. Drain. Serve at once.

Stuffed Chicken Soup

INGREDIENTS

Bird's nest	40 g (1 1/2 oz), cleaned
Chicken	1, whole, about 900 g (2 lb), bones removed and set aside
Ginger	3 slices
Salt	2 tsp
MSG	1/2 tsp, optional
Ham	1 slice, shredded

METHOD

- Soak bird's nest in cold water overnight and drain.
- Stuff the bird's nest into the chicken through the opening at the neck. Tie a string below the opening to secure.
- Bring a saucepan of water to a rapid boil and put in the chicken, ginger and 1 tsp of the salt. Cover and cook for 5 minutes.
- Remove the chicken from the stock and plunge into cold water for 5 minutes. Drain and set aside.
- Bring the stock to the boil again. Add the chicken bones and boil for 1/2 hour over high heat.
- Strain the stock and measure out 1 litre (4 1/2 cups) to be used for steaming the chicken.
- Add 1 tsp salt and 1/2 tsp MSG, if using, into the stock. Combine chicken and the seasoned stock, and steam gently for 2 hours.
- Serve hot in a deep bowl. Top with a sprinkling of shredded ham.

Braised Foreleg of Pork,
Dried Seaweed and Oysters

INGREDIENTS

Pork foreleg	1.4 kg (3 lb)
Dried Chinese mushrooms	30 g (1 oz)
Black hair moss (*fatt choy*)	15 g (1/2 oz)
Cooking oil	225 ml (1 cup)
Lard or peanut oil	4 Tbsp
Dried oysters (*ho si*)	85 g (3 oz)
Bamboo shoot	115 g (4 oz), boiled and cut into pieces
Chinese white cabbage	455 g (1 lb)
Ginger	5 slices
Garlic	3 cloves, peeled and crushed
Gingko nuts	55 g (2 oz), boiled
Water	300 ml (1 1/3 cups), boiling
Tapioca flour	1/2 tsp, mixed with 4 Tbsp water
Sesame oil	1 tsp

Marinade

Dark soy sauce	2 tsp
Sugar	2 tsp
Five-spice powder	1/2 tsp

Seasoning

Salt	1/2 tsp
Sugar	1 tsp
MSG	1 tsp, optional
Dark soy sauce	2 tsp
Soy sauce	3 tsp
Ginger juice	1 tsp
Oyster sauce	2 Tbsp

METHOD

- Marinate pork with marinade ingredients for 1/2 hour.
- Combine seasoning ingredients in another bowl and set aside.
- Wash mushrooms, cut off stems and soak in hot water until soft. Halve the mushrooms and set aside. Reserve the mushroom water for later use.
- Wash black hair moss thoroughly to remove grit and sand. Soak in hot water until soft.
- Heat wok with cooking oil until very hot. Add pork and fry until golden brown, then transfer pork to a small non-stick saucepan. Add 115 ml (1/2 cup) boiling water to the pork and simmer until tender.
- In a clean wok, heat 2 Tbsp lard or peanut oil. Fry black hair moss, mushrooms, dried oysters, bamboo shoot and Chinese cabbage separately. Transfer to a dish.
- Add the remaining lard or cooking oil and fry ginger and garlic until light brown. Return the fried ingredients into the wok with the gingko nuts and seasoning. Stir-fry for a moment.
- Transfer the mixture into a heavy-bottomed saucepan. Add the braised pork and gravy, 300 ml (1 1/3 cups) boiling water and cook gently, covered, for 45 minutes.
- Stir in the tapioca flour mixture and lastly, the sesame oil. Serve hot.

Braised Beef Brisket

INGREDIENTS

Beef brisket	680 g (1 1/2 lb), thickly sliced
Cooking oil	2 Tbsp
Lettuce	455 g (1 lb), sliced into large pieces

Marinade

Water	570 ml (2 1/2 cups)
Dark soy sauce	2 Tbsp
Soy sauce	2 Tbsp
MSG	1 tsp, optional
Sugar	1 tsp
Vinegar	2 tsp
Pepper	1 tsp

Aromatics

Garlic	3 cloves, peeled and crushed
Star anise	2 segments
Shallots	4, peeled and crushed
Ginger	4 slices, peeled
Galangal	2 thick slices, peeled
Lemon grass	2 stalks, crushed

METHOD

- Combine marinade ingredients and marinate beef for 1/2 hour.
- Heat cooking oil in a claypot until very hot. Add aromatics and stir-fry for 2 minutes.
- Add the marinated beef, together with the remaining marinade and bring to the boil over high heat for 10 minutes. Reduce heat, cover and simmer for 1 1/2–2 hours or until beef is tender.
- To serve, arrange lettuce on a serving plate and place beef on top. Serve hot.

Note
Alternatively, this dish can be served up in a claypot as shown in the picture.

Barbecued Pork Spareribs

INGREDIENTS

Pork spareribs	900 g (2 lb), chopped, washed and drained
Lard	4 Tbsp
Cucumbers	4, sliced

Marinade

Tomato sauce	2 Tbsp
Sugar	2 Tbsp
Sweet chilli sauce	1 Tbsp
Sherry or brandy	1 Tbsp
Soy sauce	2 Tbsp
Lime juice	$^1/_2$ Tbsp
MSG	1 Tbsp, optional
Pepper	1 tsp

METHOD

- Combine marinade ingredients in a bowl. Set aside.
- Dry spareribs with a tea towel, then marinate it for 4 hours.
- Thread pieces of the meat onto skewers. Set aside remaining marinade for basting later.
- Line baking tray with foil to collect the juices.
- Brush sparerib pieces with lard, and grill or bake them at 230°C (450°F) for 10 minutes.
- Turn over the meat once. Reduce the heat to 150°C (300°F) and cook for a further 15–20 minutes.
- Combine the drippings and remaining marinade and baste often.
- When meat is done, serve with cucumber slices.

Wee Seet

SCRAMBLED EGGS WITH CRABMEAT AND SHARK'S FIN

INGREDIENTS

Eggs	10
Cooking oil	2 Tbsp
Salt	1 tsp
MSG	1 tsp, optional
Pepper	1/2 tsp
Soy sauce	1 Tbsp
Crabmeat	115 g (4 oz)
Shark's fin	115 g (4 oz), processed
Belly pork	115 g (4 oz), thinly shredded
Prawns	115 g (4 oz), shelled
Spring onions	30 g (1 oz), cut into 4-cm (1 1/2-in) lengths
Water	3 Tbsp
Sesame oil	1 tsp
Lard or cooking oil	6 Tbsp

METHOD

- In a bowl, combine eggs, 2 Tbsp cooking oil, salt, MSG, if using, pepper and soy sauce and beat until frothy.
- Stir in crabmeat, shark's fin, pork, prawns, spring onions and water.
- In another bowl, combine sesame oil and lard or cooking oil and set aside.
- Heat a wok until very hot, then pour in half the oil mixture. When hot, add in half of the egg mixture and fry over high heat, cutting scrambled eggs into bite-sized pieces as you fry. Cook until light brown.
- Transfer to a serving plate and repeat with remaining egg mixture.
- Serve hot.

Note:
Processed and treated shark's fin is available at supermarkets and some wet markets. If they are not available, soak shark's fin in warm water with about 1–2 Tbsp lye water overnight to allow fins to soften and swell.

Loh Hon Chye

MIXED VEGETABLES

INGREDIENTS

Mustard greens (*gai choy*)	455 g (1 lb), stalks only
Water	850 ml (3³/₄ cups), boiling
Sugar	2 tsp
Cooking oil	1 Tbsp
Salt	¹/₂ tsp
Bicarbonate of soda	¹/₂ tsp
Lard or cooking oil	115 g (4 oz)
Ginger	6 slices, peeled
Garlic	¹/₂ tsp, peeled and pounded
Dried Chinese mushrooms	6–8, soaked and quartered
Snow peas	115 g (4 oz), blanched
Young corn cobs	¹/₂ can, halved and drained
Bamboo shoots	115 g (4 oz), sliced
Button mushrooms	¹/₂ can, halved and drained
Gingko nuts	1 handful, boiled for ¹/₂ hour until soft
Mock abalone	¹/₂ can
Chicken stock	455 ml (2 cups)
Tapioca flour or cornflour	1¹/₂ Tbsp, mixed with 4 Tbsp water

Seasoning

Soy sauce	2 tsp
MSG	1 tsp, optional
Seasme oil	¹/₂ tsp
Sugar	1 tsp
Oyster sauce	2 Tbsp

METHOD

- Cook the mustard greens first. Cut the thick stems into large pieces and plunge into boiling water, adding sugar, cooking oil, salt and bicarbonate of soda.
- Bring the water back to a fast boil for 3 minutes, then remove the vegetable. Refresh in a generous bowl of cold water briefly. Drain and chill in the refrigerator until ready for use.
- Heat a wok until very hot and add 2 Tbsp of the lard or cooking oil. When hot, fry the ginger and garlic until light brown, then toss in the Chinese mushrooms and snow peas. Fry for a moment, then transfer to a bowl.
- Add another 2 Tbsp of lard or oil and stir-fry the corn, bamboo shoots, button mushrooms, gingko nuts and mock abalone for ¹/₂ minute. Add the seasoning ingredients, chicken stock and the rest of the ingredients (except the mustard greens and tapioca flour solution). Bring to the boil.
- Now add the mustard greens, cover and return to a boil. Stir in the tapioca flour solution.
- When sauce has thickened a little, serve up the vegetables in a large serving plate.

tokpanjang

FESTIVE COOKING – THE BEST OF SINGAPORE'S RECIPES

Turmeric and Yoghurt Chicken

INGREDIENTS

Chicken	1.4 kg (3 lb), cut into large pieces
Salt	1 level Tbsp
Sugar	1 tsp
MSG	1 tsp, optional
Yoghurt	55 g (2 oz)
Evaporated milk	285 ml (1 1/4 cups)
Shallots or onions	115 g (4 oz), peeled
Garlic	2 cloves, peeled
Ginger	4 slices, peeled
Ghee	85 g (3 oz)
Water	455 ml (2 cups), hot
Tomatoes	2, thickly sliced
Green chillies	2, thickly sliced

Seasoning

Salt	1 1/2 tsp
Sugar	2 tsp
MSG	1 tsp, optional

Spice mix

Ground coriander	2 Tbsp
Ground cumin	2 Tbsp
Ground aniseed	1 tsp
Ground cinnamon	1/4 tsp
Ground turmeric	1 tsp

METHOD

- Marinate chicken with salt, sugar and MSG, if using, and leave for 1/2 hour.
- Combine yoghurt, evaporated milk, seasoning and spice mix in a bowl and blend. Rub chicken with this mixture and leave aside for 20 minutes.
- Pound shallots or onions, garlic and ginger into a fine paste and set aside.
- Heat a heavy-bottomed saucepan, then add ghee. When hot, fry pounded shallot mixture until light brown and fragrant. Add 225 ml (1 cup) of hot water and bring to the boil.
- Add the chicken mixture and cook over moderate heat for about 20 minutes or until chicken is done and gravy is thick. Stir occasionally to prevent burning.
- Add remaining water, tomatoes and green chillies. Cover and simmer for 15–20 minutes or until chicken is tender.
- Serve hot.

Chicken Mulligatawny

INGREDIENTS

Chicken	1.4 kg (3 lb), cleaned
Water	2.5 litres (10 cups)
Salt	2 tsp
MSG	1 tsp, optional
Peppercorns	2 tsp
Ghee	3 Tbsp (or 1 1/2 Tbsp cooking oil, mixed with 1 1/2 Tbsp butter)
Ginger	1 tsp, peeled and chopped
Shallots	115 g (4 oz), peeled and sliced
Cloves	3
Cinnamon quill	4-cm (1 1/2-in) piece
Curry powder	1 Tbsp
Garlic	2 tsp, peeled and chopped
Curry leaves (*daun kari*)	1 sprig
Celery	1 stalk, sliced thickly
Lemon juice	2 Tbsp
Cooked rice	2 cups, cooled
Crisp-fried shallots	1/2 cup (*recipe on page 12*)

METHOD

- Place chicken in a stock pot with water, salt, MSG, if using, and peppercorns. Boil over high heat for 10 minutes, skimming off the scum as it rises.
- Pour in another cup of cold water and bring it to the boil again. Reduce heat and simmer for 1/2 hour. Remove chicken and plunge into cold water for 5 minutes, then cut it into pieces and debone.
- Return chicken bones to the stock to boil for another hour over moderate heat. Strain stock and set aside.
- In a pan, heat ghee and fry ginger and sliced shallots until light brown. Add cloves, cinnamon, curry powder, chopped garlic and curry leaves and stir-fry for a minute.
- Transfer stock into a saucepan and add in the fried mixture. Add celery and bring to the boil. Reduce heat to a gentle boil for 10 minutes.
- Lastly, add lemon juice and remove from heat.
- To serve: Fill small soup bowls with chicken and rice. Add the soup and top with crisp-fried shallots and a dash of pepper.

Beef Serondeng

BEEF WITH GRATED COCONUT

INGREDIENTS

Water	115 ml ($^1/_2$ cup)
Rump or Scotch steak	560 g (1 $^1/_4$ lb), cut into pieces
Cooking oil	6 Tbsp
Coconut	560 g (1 $^1/_4$ lb), skinned and coarsely grated

Rempah

Galangal	6 slices, peeled
Shallots	14, peeled
Coriander seeds	4 Tbsp
Cumin seeds	1 tsp
Ginger	4 slices, peeled
Garlic	3 cloves, peeled
Turmeric	2 slices, peeled
Pepper	1 tsp

Seasoning

Salt	1 Tbsp
Sugar	5 Tbsp
Palm sugar (*gula Melaka*)	3 Tbsp, grated
Tamarind pulp (*asam*)	55 g (2 oz), mixed with 8 Tbsp water, squeezed and strained

METHOD

- Place *rempah* ingredients in a mortar and pestle and pound into a paste. Set aside.
- Bring 115 ml ($^1/_2$ cup) of water to the boil in a pan. Add beef, one-third of the *rempah* paste and simmer until beef is tender and almost dry. Set aside.
- Heat 4 Tbsp of cooking oil in a wok and stir-fry the remaining *rempah* paste until fragrant.
- Add seasoning ingredients, stir-fry for a minute more and transfer to a dish. Rub fried paste into the grated coconut.
- Heat the remaining 2 Tbsp oil in a pan. Add the coconut mixture and the beef and stir-fry over low heat until moist and fragrant. (Stir often to prevent the coconut from burning.)
- When done, transfer to a plate and serve.

Indonesian Satay

Satay

INGREDIENTS

Coriander seeds	3 Tbsp
Cumin seeds	1 tsp
Galangal	12 thin slices, peeled
Lemon grass	3 stalks, thinly sliced
Lemon juice	$1/2$ Tbsp
Palm sugar (*gula Melaka*)	2 Tbsp, grated
Sugar	1 tsp
Salt	1 level tsp
Cooking oil	2 Tbsp
Lean pork or rump steak	570 g ($4^1/4$ lb), chilled, thinly sliced
Water	4 Tbsp, mixed with another 2 Tbsp cooking oil

METHOD

- Fry coriander and cumin seeds over very low heat for 5 minutes or toast under a low grill. When heated through, pound in a dry mortar until fine. Set aside.
- Pound galangal and lemon grass into a paste. Place in a bowl and mix with the coriander and cumin, lemon juice, palm sugar, sugar, salt and cooking oil. Marinate pork in this for 1 hour.
- Thread pork onto wooden sticks or metal skewers.
- Grill over hot coals or under a grill until done, turning the satay to ensure even cooking. Baste often with water and oil.
- Serve with Indonesian Tangy Sauce.

Indonesian Tangy Sauce

INGREDIENTS

Sweet Indonesian sauce	140 ml ($2/3$ cup)
Green bird's eye chillies	10, halved
Red bird's eye chillies	10, halved
Lime (*limau nipis*) juice	4 Tbsp
Lime rind	from $1/2$ lime, thinly sliced

METHOD

- Combine all ingredients in a bowl and blend. Serve on the side with Indonesian satay.

Note:
Sweet Indonesian sauce can be bought from supermarkets. If unavailable, combine 285 ml ($1^1/4$ cups) best quality dark soy sauce with 225 ml (1 cup) golden syrup and boil gently for 20 minutes. Keep in a clean dry bottle for future use.

Kurma Kambing

MUTTON KURMA

INGREDIENTS

Mutton	900 g (2 lb), cut into large cubes
Ginger juice	1 Tbsp
Salt	1 tsp
Ghee	4 Tbsp, or 2 Tbsp butter, mixed with 3 Tbsp cooking oil
Shallots	115 g (4 oz), peeled and thinly sliced
Water	125 ml (1/2 cup)
Chinese parsley (coriander leaves)	2 stalks, with roots
Yoghurt	4 Tbsp

Rempah

Shallots	55 g (2 oz), peeled
Garlic	2 cloves, peeled
Ginger	20 g (3/4 oz), peeled
Cashew nuts	55 g (2 oz)
Green chillies	4

Spice Mix

Ground coriander	3 tsp
Ground cumin	1 1/2 tsp
Ground cinnamon	1/2 tsp
Ground cloves	1/2 tsp, or 6 cloves, finely pounded
Ground pepper	1 tsp
Ground turmeric	1/2 tsp
Cooking oil	4 Tbsp

Seasoning

Salt	1 1/2–2 tsp
Sugar	1 tsp
MSG	1 tsp, optional

METHOD

- Combine *rempah* ingredients in a mortar and pestle and pound into a fine paste. Set aside.
- Marinate mutton with the ginger juice, salt and one-third of the *rempah* paste and leave aside for 1 hour.
- Place spice mix ingredients in a frying pan and toast over very low heat for 5 minutes until fragrant. Set aside.
- Heat ghee in a heavy-bottomed saucepan and fry sliced shallots until light brown. Transfer shallots to a plate, leaving the oil in the pan.
- Add the remaining *rempah* paste and fry until fragrant and oil bubbles through. Add spice mix and stir-fry for 1/2 minute. Stir in water and seasoning, and cook until paste is fragrant.
- Add marinated mutton and Chinese parsley stalks, and cook for 10 minutes over moderately high heat. Add yoghurt, then reduce heat to low. Cover and simmer for 1–1 1/2 hours or until meat is tender. Stir occasionally to prevent burning. Add a little water if gravy becomes too thick before the meat is tender.

Beef Merah

BEEF IN RED SPICY SAUCE

INGREDIENTS

Beef	900 g (2 lb), cubed
Ghee	115 g (4 oz)
Ginger	1 tsp, peeled and thinly sliced
Shallots	115 g (4 oz), peeled and thinly sliced
Chilli powder	3 Tbsp
Tomato paste	3 Tbsp
Yoghurt	4 Tbsp
Water	170 ml ($^3/_4$ cup)
Tomatoes	170 g (6 oz), quartered

Marinade

Ground coriander	3 Tbsp
Ground cumin	2 Tbsp
Pepper	$1^1/_4$ tsp
Milk	115 ml ($^1/_2$ cup)
Onions	85 g (3 oz), peeled and thinly sliced
Ground ginger	1 tsp, or ginger juice
Sugar	3 tsp
MSG	1 tsp, optional
Salt	2 tsp
Lime juice	1 tsp

METHOD

- Marinate beef with marinade ingredients for 45 minutes.
- In a heated saucepan or wok, add ghee and fry the ginger until brown. Add the shallots and continue frying until light brown.
- Now add the chilli powder, tomato paste and yoghurt and stir over low heat until fragrant and oil turns red.
- Add the water and bring to the boil. Increase heat to moderately high and add in the beef. Cook for $^1/_2$ hour, stirring occasionally. Reduce heat to low, then add the tomatoes.
- Cover and cook for 45 minutes to 1 hour or until meat is tender and gravy is thick. Transfer to a dish and serve.

Note:
Add a little water if the gravy becomes too thick before the meat is tender.

Long Beans and Prawns in Coconut Sauce

INGREDIENTS

Coconut	455 g (1 lb), grated
Water	115 ml (1/2 cup) for No.2 coconut milk
Cooking oil	3 Tbsp
Salt	1 tsp
Sugar	2 tsp
Prawns	455 g (1 lb), washed and shelled (keep shells for stock)
Long beans	280 g (10 oz), finely sliced

Rempah

Shallots	85 g (3 oz), peeled
Garlic	1 clove, peeled
Candlenuts	3
Red chilli	1, small, seeded
Lemon grass	1 stalk, bruised

METHOD

- Using a piece of muslin, squeeze grated coconut to extract No.1 milk. Set aside. Add water to the grated coconut and squeeze again for No.2 milk. Collect separately.
- Combine *rempah* ingredients and pound or blend into a fine paste.
- Heat cooking oil in a wok and fry *rempah* paste until fragrant and oil separates.
- Add salt, sugar and half of the No.1 milk. Cook for 1 minute.
- Add prawns and stir over moderately high heat until prawns change colour.
- Add long beans and stir in No. 2 milk. Cook for 5 minutes or until beans are tender.
- Pour in remaining No.1 milk, reduce heat and cook for another 1–2 minutes. Serve.

Chap Chye Masak Titik

STEWED VEGETABLES NYONYA STYLE

INGREDIENTS

Belly pork	250 g (9 oz)
Salt	1/4 tsp
Water	750 ml (3 1/2 cups)
Prawns	250 g (9 oz)
Cloud ear fungus (*bok nee*)	30 g (1 oz), soaked in warm water
Golden needles (*kim chiam*)	60 g (2 oz)
Cellophane noodles (*tang hoon*)	30 g (1 oz), soaked in boiling water
Bean curd skin strips (*foo chok*)	60 g (2 oz), cut into lengths
Cooking oil	6 Tbsp
Sweet bean curd strips (*tim chok*)	10, cut into pieces
Yellow bean paste (*taucheo*)	2 Tbsp, pounded
Cabbage	600 g (1 lb 5 oz), sliced
Dried Chinese mushrooms	60 g (2 oz), soaked in hot water

Rempah

Shallots	120 g (4 oz), peeled
Candlenuts	4, crushed
Red chilli	1
Shrimp paste (*belacan*)	2 Tbsp

Seasoning

Salt	1 tsp
MSG	1 tsp, optional
Sugar	2 tsp

METHOD

- Place pork in a saucepan together with 1/4 tsp salt and 500 ml (2 1/4 cups) water. Boil for 20 minutes. Slice thinly and set aside. Reserve stock.
- Shell and devein prawns. Pound shells finely, stir in the remaining 250 ml (1 1/4 cups) water and strain. Set stock aside.
- Wash cloud ear fungus thoroughly to remove grit. Cut away and discard the tough base. Set aside.
- Cut off and discard hard tops of golden needles, wash and drain.
- Cut cellophane noodles into short lengths.
- Soak bean curd skin strips in cold water for 10 minutes. Drain.
- Combine *rempah* ingredients and pound to a fine paste. Set aside.
- Heat a wok. Add cooking oil and fry sweet bean curd strips over low heat until they blister and turn light brown. Set aside.
- In the same pan, fry the *rempah* paste over moderate heat until fragrant. Add yellow bean paste and seasoning and stir-fry for 2 minutes.
- Add prawns and prawn stock and bring to the boil.
- Add cabbage, cook over high heat for 5 minutes, then pour in pork stock and remaining ingredients. Continue cooking for another 15–20 minutes or until cabbage is tender.
- Serve hot.

Satay Celup

SATAY STEAMBOAT

Satay

INGREDIENTS

Rice vermicelli	225 g (8 oz)
Pork	225 g (8 oz), thinly sliced
Cockles	225 g (8 oz), shelled
Prawns	225 g (8 oz), shelled and halved lengthwise
Pork liver	225 g (8 oz), thinly sliced
Dried cuttlefish	1, soaked in alkaline water (recipe on page 12)
Water convolvulus (kangkung)	625 g (1 lb 6 oz)
Bean sprouts	455 g (1 lb), picked
Water	900 ml (4 cups), boiling

METHOD

- Scald rice vermicelli for 2 minutes. Drain and set aside.
- Thread pork, cockles, prawns, liver and cuttlefish onto wooden skewers or satay sticks.
- Blanch water convolvulus and bean sprouts. Drain and set aside.
- Place 900 ml (4 cups) boiling water in a saucepan, and add 225 ml (1 cup) of the peanut gravy (see recipe in the next column). Bring it to a simmer.
- To serve: Place single portions of water convolvulus, bean sprouts and rice vermicelli on a plate. Put the skewered ingredients in the saucepan of simmering water and let it cook gently until done.
- Serve the cooked food with the rice vermicelli and top with some of the peanut gravy.

Peanut Gravy

INGREDIENTS

Roasted peanuts	625 g (1 lb 6 oz), finely pounded
Water	900 ml (4 cups)
Cooking oil	225 ml (1 cup)
Sugar	115 g (4 oz)
Salt	1 Tbsp

Rempah

Candlenuts	10
Shallots	140 g (5 oz), peeled
Garlic	6 cloves, peeled
Lemon grass	4 stalks, sliced
Galangal	4 slices, peeled
Dried chillies	30, soaked to soften
Shrimp paste (belacan)	1 Tbsp

METHOD

- Combine rempah ingredients and pound to a fine paste. Set aside.
- Place peanuts, water and cooking oil in a saucepan and boil over low heat for 20 minutes.
- In a heated wok, add oil and fry rempah paste until fragrant and oil separates.
- Add fried rempah paste to the peanut sauce, season with sugar and salt and simmer for 10 minutes. Set aside gravy.

Note:
This recipe serves 10.

old-fashioned

FESTIVE COOKING – THE BEST OF SINGAPORE'S RECIPES

Lemon Roast Chicken

INGREDIENTS

Chicken	1.4 kg (3 lb), whole
Lard or cooking oil	4 Tbsp
Cucumber	1, sliced
Tomatoes	2, sliced
Red chillies	2, sliced

Marinade

Soy sauce	1 Tbsp
Salt	1 tsp
Sugar	1 tsp
MSG	1 tsp, optional
Pepper	$^1/_2$ tsp
Ginger juice	1 Tbsp
Sherry	$1^1/_2$ Tbsp

Gravy

Honey	2 Tbsp
Plum sauce	1 Tbsp
Apricot jam	2 Tbsp
Lemon juice	2 Tbsp
Sherry	1 tsp

METHOD

- Wash chicken and wipe dry thoroughly.
- In a bowl, combine all the marinade ingredients except for $^1/_2$ Tbsp sherry.
- Take 1 Tbsp of the marinade mixture and blend with the $^1/_2$ Tbsp sherry. Rub this mixture onto the inside of chicken. Rub the rest of the marinade all over surface of the chicken and leave for 1 hour.
- Rub chicken with 2 Tbsp lard or cooking oil, then roast it in the oven at 175°C (350°F) for 35–40 minutes or until done.
- Remove chicken from the oven to cool, then cut into pieces. Set aside pan juices.
- Now prepare the gravy: Heat 2 Tbsp lard or cooking oil until hot. Pour in gravy ingredients and bring to boil over low heat for $^1/_2$ minute.
- Garnish chicken with sliced cucumber, tomatoes and chillies. Pour gravy over chicken and serve.

Chicken, Pineapple and Chestnut Casserole

INGREDIENTS

Chicken	1.6 kg (3½ lb), washed and cut into large pieces
Self-raising flour	225 g (8 oz)
Cooking oil	2 Tbsp
Butter	2 Tbsp
Button mushrooms	1 small can
Pineapple rings	1 can, or 4–6 rings
Small or pickling onions	8–10, peeled
Plain flour	1 Tbsp
Pineapple juice	170 ml (¾ cup)
Water	115 ml (½ cup)
Roasted or canned chestnuts	225 g (8 oz)
Cooking oil for deep-frying	500 ml (2¼ cups)

Marinade

Salt	1 tsp
Sugar	1 tsp
Pepper	1 tsp

Seasoning

Salt	1 tsp
Dark soy sauce	1 Tbsp
Chicken stock cube	1
Sugar	1 tsp

METHOD

- Marinate chicken with the salt, sugar and pepper for ½ hour.
- Coat chicken pieces with self-raising flour.
- Heat some cooking oil in a wok and brown the chicken pieces. Transfer to a metal sieve and drain. Set aside.
- Clean the wok and add the butter and 2 Tbsp oil. Fry button mushrooms and pineapple rings for 2 minutes, then set aside.
- In the same wok, fry onions for 5 minutes until transparent. Add plain flour and stir-fry for a moment. Pour in pineapple juice and water, seasoning and chestnuts. Cook, covered, over low heat for 20 minutes.
- Transfer chicken, gravy and the rest of the wok's contents into a deep casserole dish. Cook covered in an oven at 170–200°C (325–400°F) for 1–1½ hours.
- Finally, add the mushrooms and pineapple rings. Continue cooking for another 10–15 minutes. Serve hot.

Roast Turkey with Pork and Rice Filling

INGREDIENTS

Turkey	$3^1/_2$–4 kg ($7^1/_2$–$8^1/_4$ lb), whole
Sherry	2 Tbsp
Salt	1 tsp
Pepper	$^1/_2$ tsp
Butter	3 Tbsp, softened

Marinade

Salt	1 Tbsp
Pepper	1 tsp
Honey	1 tsp
Soy sauce	1 tsp

Filling

Bacon	2 slices, roughly chopped
Butter	55 g (2 oz)
Onions	60 g (2 oz), peeled and chopped
Minced pork	340 g (12 oz)
Cooked rice	3 cups
Chicken stock cube	1, crushed in 4 Tbsp boiling water
Chinese parsley	$^1/_2$ cup, roughly chopped
Sultanas	$^3/_4$ cup
Almonds	$^1/_2$ cup, blanched, toasted and coarsely chopped
Ham	120 g (4 oz)

METHOD

- Wash the turkey and pat dry with a kitchen towel.
- Rub the inside of the cavity with sherry, salt and pepper, then brush the entire turkey with butter.
- Now rub the marinade ingredients all over the turkey and set aside for $^1/_2$ hour.
- Prepare the filling: Dry-fry the bacon in a pan until crispy and set aside. Add butter to the same pan and fry the onions until soft. Add minced pork and stir-fry until pork changes colour. Stir in the cooked rice and chicken stock solution. Add parsley, sultanas, almonds and ham and mix well.
- Loosely stuff the turkey with the filling. Remember to leave some space in the cavity as the filling will expand during cooking.
- Secure the cavity with a skewer. Brush again with more butter. Cross the ends of the drumsticks and tie with some string.
- Place the turkey on a rack over a baking tray lined with foil to catch the drippings.
- Roast turkey in a pre-heated oven at 220°C (425°F) for $2^1/_2$– 3 hours. Reduce heat after turkey turns light brown and continue cooking until golden brown.
- Baste turkey with drippings regularly. Use foil to cover the parts of the turkey that brown too quickly.
- When done, set the turkey aside to cool for 15–20 minutes before carving.

Note:
Excess filling can be pressed into patties, wrapped in foil and baked with the turkey.

Add 112 ml ($^1/_2$ cup) water to the baking tray to prevent drippings from scorching. Add more water if gravy dries up too quickly.

Gammon with Pineapple

INGREDIENTS

Gammon	1.4 kg (3 lb), middle cut
Beer	1 large bottle
Star anise	3 segments
Cinnamon quill	2.5-cm (1-in) piece
Cloves	6
Palm sugar (*gula Melaka*)	30 g (1 oz)
Brown sugar	2 Tbsp
Honey	1 Tbsp
Mustard	1 tsp
Juice of one orange	
Pineapple rings	1 small can, drained
Cucumber slices	

METHOD

- Place gammon in a large saucepan with beer, star anise, cinnamon quill, cloves and palm sugar. Bring to the boil over moderate heat for 1–1¹⁄₂ hours or until meat is tender.
- Leave to cool for 1 hour. Drain and transfer meat to a roasting pan.
- Combine brown sugar, honey, mustard and orange juice in a pan and heat gently until sugar dissolves and mixture takes on the consistency of a glaze.
- Remove skin from the gammon. Coat the meat with the sugar glaze and bake in a 175°C (350°F) oven for 20 minutes.
- Remove gammon from the oven and place pineapple rings around the meat. Return meat to the oven and bake for another 10 minutes until golden brown. Baste meat with juices from the pan occasionally.
- Remove from oven and let cool.
- Chill in the refrigerator if gammon is to be served as a cold dish. Garnish with cucumber slices

Baked Crayfish Mornay

INGREDIENTS

Butter	50 g (1 1/2 oz)
Cooking oil	1 Tbsp
Onions	85 g (3 oz), peeled and sliced
Celery	4 Tbsp, thinly sliced
Plain flour	2 heaped Tbsp
Milk	285 ml (1 1/4 cups)
Crayfish meat	340 g (12 oz), cooked and chopped
Egg whites	2, lightly beaten
Mozzarella cheese	115 g (4 oz), coarsely grated

Seasoning

Sugar	1/2 tsp
Salt	1/4 tsp
Pepper	1/2 tsp

Topping

Breadcrumbs	1/2 cup
Salami	140 g (5 oz), chopped
Mozzarella cheese	100 g (3 1/2 oz), coarsely grated

METHOD

- Heat the butter and cooking oil in a pan and fry onions and celery until soft and transparent.
- Stir in the flour, add the milk and blend.
- Reduce heat to low and add crayfish, seasoning and egg whites. Cook for a minute, then add the cheese. Stir and remove from heat.
- Grease a deep, oven-proof dish and dust with flour. Pour in crayfish mixture. Layer the top with half of the breadcrumbs, followed by the salami and the 100 g (3 1/2 oz) cheese. Spread the remaining breadcrumbs on top.
- Bake in an oven at about 120°C (250°F) for 1/2 hour. Serve hot.

Brandy Alexandra

INGREDIENTS

Digestive biscuits	185 g (6 oz)
Butter	115 g (4 oz)
Marshmallows	100 g (3 oz)
Milk	2 Tbsp
Brandy	2 Tbsp
Coffee liqueur	1 Tbsp
Gelatine	2 tsp, dissolved in 2 Tbsp hot water
Cream	300 ml (1 1/3 cups)
Dark chocolate	55 g (2 oz), flaked

METHOD

- Crush biscuits until fine. Melt the butter and mix into the crushed biscuits.
- Grease a 20-cm (8-in) flan tin (*see picture below*) with butter. Firmly press a layer of the pounded biscuits to the bottom and sides of the tin. Chill.
- Melt marshmallows in a pan with 2 Tbsp milk over low heat. Add brandy, coffee liqueur and melted gelatine and stir to blend.
- Whip the cream until thick and mix it into the marshmallow mixture. Pour into flan tin and chill.
- Decorate flan with chocolate flakes before serving.

White Christmas

MIXED FRUIT AND COCONUT CANDY BARS

INGREDIENTS

Icing sugar	250 g (9 oz), sifted
Full cream milk powder	250 g (9 oz), sifted
Desiccated coconut	250 g (9 oz), toasted lightly
Mixed fruit	250 g (9 oz)
Rice crispies	2 cups
Walnuts	65 g (2 oz), coarsely chopped
Almonds	65 g (2 oz), toasted and coarsely chopped
Copha	250 g (9 oz)
Vanilla essence	1 tsp

METHOD

- Combine all the ingredients except the copha and vanilla essence in a mixing bowl.
- Place copha in a heavy-bottomed pan and heat until just melted. Add vanilla essence.
- Pour copha mixture into the fruit and nut mixture and stir until well combined.
- Pour mixture into a lightly greased baking pan (measuring 24 x 18 cm [9^1/$_2$ x 7^1/$_4$ in]) or glass baking dish (*picture on this page*). With the back of a spoon, press the mixture down firmly and smoothen the top to level the surface.
- Chill in the refrigerator for at least 2 hours before cutting it into fingers. Store in refrigerator.

Note:
Copha is solid cream of coconut available in specialty stores. You can also use packaged desiccated coconut.

Christmas Cake

INGREDIENTS

Brandy	3 Tbsp
Plain flour	250 g (9 oz)
Self-raising flour	60 g (2 oz)
Salt	1 level tsp
Mixed spice	1/2 tsp *(see below)*
Butter	250 g (9 oz), diced and slightly chilled
Brown sugar	200 g (7 oz)
Honey	2 Tbsp, chilled
Vanilla essence	1 tsp
Almond essence	4 drops, optional
Eggs	5, chilled

Dried Fruits and Nuts

Currants	225 g (8 oz)
Sultanas	225 g (8 oz), chopped
Raisins	225 g (8 oz), chopped
Mixed peel	125 g (4 1/2 oz), coarsely chopped
Glazed cherries	115 g (4 oz), sliced
Almonds	125 g (4 1/2 oz), blanched, coarsely chopped
Walnuts	115 g (4 oz), coarsely chopped

METHOD

- Grease and line a cake tin with greaseproof paper, and grease the paper as well.
- Place the dried fruits and nuts in a mixing bowl and add in the brandy. Let it soak for 1/2 hour.
- Combine the plain flour, self-raising flour, salt and mixed spice and sift twice.
- Set aside 2 Tbsp of flour mixture for use later. Rub the rest of the flour into the fruit and nut mixture.
- In another bowl, use a blender to cream the butter and brown sugar together until mixture becomes light and fluffy. Add honey, vanilla essence and almond essence and beat for 5 minutes.
- Now add the eggs one at a time. Increase the speed of the blender and mix until the egg is well combined, then reduce the speed to normal and beat for another 5 minutes. Finally, add in the reserved 2 Tbsp flour.
- Add the flour and fruit mixture to the egg mixture and stir until it is well blended.
- Spoon the batter into the prepared cake tin. Level surface and make a dent in the middle. Bake at about 200°C (400°F) for 15 minutes. Reduce to 180°C (350°F) and continue baking until done.

Mixed Spice

INGREDIENTS

Cinnamon quill	30 g (1 oz)
Cloves	20
Star anise	1
Green cardamom	20

METHOD

- Wash all the spices and dry them in the sun.
- Remove the rounded tips from the cloves.
- Fry all the spices in a heated frying pan over low heat for 20 minutes, or grill under a warm grill for 10–15 minutes.
- Remove and discard the husks from the cardamom.
- Pound the spices together until very fine, and put through a fine sieve.
- Place the spices in a clean, dry bottle and store in the refrigerator for future use.

festivespecialties

FESTIVE COOKING – THE BEST OF SINGAPORE'S RECIPES

Yue Sang

CANTONESE RAW FISH SALAD

INGREDIENTS

Chinese radish (*daikon*)	455 g (1 lb)
Sweet potatoes	115 g (4 oz)
Carrots	115 g (4 oz)
Sweet crisp flakes	55 g (2 oz)
Wolf herring	225 g (8 oz), thinly sliced
Peanuts	55–85 g (2–3 oz), roasted and coarsely ground
Sesame seeds	4 Tbsp, toasted
Pomelo	1 small segment, or 2 Tbsp
Chinese celery	2 sprigs, short, dark green variety, cut leaves and tender stalks into short lengths
Processed jellyfish	115 g (4 oz), thinly sliced
Young ginger	30 g (1 oz), finely shredded
Preserved sweet ginger	30 g (1 oz), finely shredded
Preserved sweet red ginger	30 g (1 oz), finely shredded
Chillies	2, seeded, finely shredded
Preserved sweet and sour leeks	3, finely shredded
Lime leaves (*daun limau purut*)	2, finely shredded
Candied orange	1 small piece, finely shredded
Candied winter melon	55 g (2 oz), finely shredded

Dressing

Corn oil	4–5 Tbsp
Lime juice	2 Tbsp
Castor sugar	4 tsp
Five-spice powder	$1/4$ tsp
Fine salt	$1/2$ tsp
Pepper	$1/4$ tsp
Vinegar	3–4 Tbsp (Set aside 1 Tbsp for the fish)

METHOD

- Skin radish, sweet potatoes and carrots. Soak in cold water for an hour.
- Finely grate the radish lengthwise, soak in water and drain. Place grated radish in a piece of muslin and squeeze out excess water. Set aside in a colander to air.
- Grate sweet potatoes and immerse in water briefly. Drain immediately. Spread on a large kitchen towel and set aside on a tray.
- Grate carrots and set aside. Do not immerse in water.
- To serve, arrange all the shredded ingredients – except fish, crisp flakes and dressing - around a large round serving dish, with shredded carrot in the centre.
- Pour the reserved 1 Tbsp vinegar over it and mix well. Place fish on top of shredded carrot. Add the remaining ingredients with the fish, sprinkle dressing over and toss. Lastly, add the crispy flakes, mix again and serve.

Note:
Sweet crisp flakes are available in Chinese confectioneries in Chinatown.

To make the flakes, combine 1 egg, 1 cup water, 1 cup flour, a pinch of salt and 1 Tbsp castor sugar. Mix into a smooth batter and strain. Pour 1 Tbsp of batter at a time into the hot oil to make thin flakes; fry until light brown. Remove with a wire ladle and drain on absorbent paper. Keep in an airtight container. This can be made several days in advance.

Hu Say

CHINESE NEW YEAR RAW FISH SALAD TEOCHEW STYLE

INGREDIENTS

Fish fillet	455 g (1 lb), preferably wolf herring. sashimi grade
Lettuce	225 g (8 oz), thickly sliced
Cucumber	2, halved lengthwise, then thinly sliced
Young ginger	10 g, or about $1/2$ Tbsp, finely shredded
Chinese celery	3 stalks, sliced
Sesame seeds	1 Tbsp, for garnishing

Dressing

Roasted peanuts	225 g (8 oz), ground
Sugar	2 Tbsp
Sweet chilli sauce	4 Tbsp
Vinegar	2 Tbsp
Kalamansi lime (*limau kesturi*) juice	2 Tbsp
Plum paste	8 Tbsp
Soy sauce	1 level tsp
Sesame oil	4 Tbsp

METHOD

- Have the fishmonger slice the fish very thinly.
- To make the dressing, combine roasted peanuts, sugar and chilli sauce in a bowl. Then add vinegar, kalamansi lime juice, plum paste, soy sauce and sesame oil. Blend well.
- To serve, arrange vegetables on a large serving plate: lettuce first, followed by the cucumber, fish, sliced ginger and Chinese celery. Sprinkle sesame seeds over and pour on the dressing just before serving.

Vegetable Dumplings

INGREDIENTS

Dried Chinese mushrooms	55 g (2 oz)
Peanut oil	6 Tbsp
Garlic	2 tsp, peeled and pounded
Ginger	2 tsp, peeled and finely chopped
Onion	115 g (4 oz), peeled and diced
Button mushrooms	225 g (8 oz), diced
Jicama (*bangkuang* or *yam bean*)	455 g (1 lb), peeled and diced
Prepared gluten (mock duck)	225 g (8 oz), diced
Sweet bean curd strips (*tim chok*)	55 g (2 oz), diced
Carrots	115 g (4 oz), skinned and diced

Seasoning

Sugar	3 Tbsp
Salt	1 tsp
MSG	1 1/2 tsp, optional
Dark soy sauce	4 tsp
Soy sauce	2 tsp
Sherry	1 tsp
Sesame oil	1 tsp

Thickening

Plain flour	2 Tbsp
Cooking oil	2 Tbsp
Water	8 Tbsp

Dough

Self-raising flour	225 g (8 oz)
Icing sugar	3 Tbsp
Baking powder	2 tsp
Cooking oil	2 Tbsp
Vinegar	1 tsp
Milk	130 ml (2/3 cup)

METHOD

To make the filling

- Rinse Chinese mushrooms and soak in 255 ml (1 cup) boiling water to soften. Retain soaking water for stock.
- Combine all seasoning ingredients in a bowl and set aside.
- Heat peanut oil in a pan until hot and fry garlic and ginger until light brown. Add onion and stir-fry until soft and transparent.
- Add button and Chinese mushrooms and stir-fry for 1/2 minute. Add jicama, gluten, bean curd strips and carrots and stir. Add seasoning and half of the mushroom water. Cook for 10 minutes over moderate heat.
- Add in remaining mushroom water and simmer until gravy is reduced and mixture is almost dry.
- Blend thickening ingredients in a bowl and stir into the pan of vegetables. Cook for another 1/2 minute. (Add a few spoonfuls of water if mixture is too dry.)
- Transfer to a bowl and chill before use.

To prepare the dough

- Sift flour, sugar and baking powder together into a mixing bowl.
- In a separate bowl, blend together oil, vinegar and milk.
- Make a well in the centre of the flour and pour in the milk mixture. Stir until mixture is combined to form a dough.
- Transfer dough to a lightly floured board or flat surface and knead lightly until smooth.
- Cut dough into 2 portions and roll each into a log. Cut into smaller, equal pieces, then cover with a cloth to prevent them from drying out.

To assemble dumpling

- Take a piece of dough and flatten with a rolling pin. Place 2 Tbsp of chilled filling in centre and pull up the sides of the dough to enclose. Pleat and press with fingers to seal.
- Place a square of greaseproof paper under each dumpling and set aside. Repeat with remaining ingredients.
- Steam dumplings over rapidly boiling water for 10 minutes. Serve hot.

Note:
Use a steamer with a tight fitting lid to prevent steam from escaping. This ensures a light textured bun.

Stewed Meat and Chestnut Dumplings

INGREDIENTS

Glutinous rice	2 kg (4 1/2 lb)
Salt	3 Tbsp
Dried bamboo leaves	1.2 kg (2 lb 11 oz), soaked overnight
Raffia string	40 pieces, each 75 cm (30 in) in length

Seasoning

Lard	280 g (10 oz)
Water	285 ml (1 1/4 cups)
Pepper	3 tsp
Five-spice powder	1 tsp
MSG	2 tsp, optional
Dark soy sauce	1 Tbsp

Filling

Dried chestnuts	400 g (14 oz)
Streaky pork	1.6 kg (3 1/2 lb), cubed
Dark soy sauce	2 Tbsp
Sugar	5 Tbsp
Pepper	1/2 tsp
Salt	1 tsp
MSG	1 tsp, optional
Five-spice powder	1 tsp
Dried Chinese mushrooms	85 g (3 oz)
Lard	6 Tbsp
Shallots	115 g (4 oz), peeled and thinly sliced
Garlic	5 cloves, peeled and coarsely pounded
Yellow bean paste (taucheo)	2 Tbsp, ground
Water	340 ml (1 1/2 cups)

METHOD

- Soak glutinous rice overnight in salt water. Drain and set aside.
- Combine seasoning ingredients in a wok and bring to the boil. Add glutinous rice and stir until liquid is absorbed. Transfer to a large bowl and set aside.

To make the filling.

- Soak chestnuts in cold water for an hour, then place in a saucepan and boil until tender.
- Marinate pork cubes with dark soy sauce, 4 Tbsp sugar, pepper, salt, MSG, if using, and five-spice powder for an hour.
- Soak Chinese mushrooms in hot water and remove stalks. Cut into large cubes.
- Heat lard in a wok and fry shallots and garlic until light brown. Add the yellow bean paste, 1 Tbsp sugar and fry until fragrant, adding spoonfuls of water in the process.
- Add in pork mixture and fry over moderate heat until almost dry. Add remaining water and bring to the boil. Reduce heat, cover pan and cook until pork is almost tender, between 45 minutes to an hour.
- Put in mushrooms and chestnuts and cook until meat is tender and dry. Set aside to cool.

To wrap dumplings

- Take two bamboo leaves and fold into a cone. Scoop 2–3 Tbsp glutinous rice into the cone, spreading and pressing rice firmly towards the bottom and sides of the cone.
- Fill with stewed pork mixture, cover the filling with more rice. Fold leaves over and secure with a length of raffia.
- When all the dumplings are assembled, tie them together in bunches of six.

To cook dumplings

- Place some water in a deep saucepan with 2 Tbsp salt. Bring to the boil. Put in dumplings and boil over high heat for 2 hours. (Replenish with more boiling water as the water evaporates.)
- When dumplings are cooked, remove them from the saucepan and hang to allow moisture to run off.
- Dumplings are best served after they have cooled and glutinous rice holds together.
- To reheat before serving, steam dumplings, but never reboil.

Note:
To test if the dumplings are cooked, unwrap one and check if the glutinous rice is smooth. Continue cooking if it is not yet done.

Kee Chung

GLUTINOUS RICE DUMPLINGS

INGREDIENTS

Glutinous rice	1.2 kg (2 lb 11 oz), remove transparent grains
Salt	2 tsp
Alkaline water	4 Tbsp (recipe on page 13, and also available at specialty bakery supply shops)
Bamboo leaves (fresh or dried)	60, washed and drained
Raffia string	40–50 long strands (soaked overnight and tied together in equal lengths)
Borax	1 tsp (available at Chinese dispensaries)

METHOD

- Wash glutinous rice until water runs clear. Drain.
- Put the glutinous rice in a porcelain container, add 1 tsp of salt and 2 Tbsp of alkaline water and mix. Add enough water to cover up to 2.5 cm (1 in) above the level of the glutinous rice. Soak overnight, or for at least 12 hours.
- Drain and transfer to an enamel or porcelain bowl. Add in the rest of the alkaline water and mix well. Set aside for 1/2 hour.

To wrap and boil the dumplings

- Take 1 broad long bamboo leaf or 2 narrow leaves and fold into a cone.
- Place 3 Tbsp glutinous rice in the cone and fold the leaf over the rice to form a triangular shape. Use raffia string to tie securely around the dumpling, then tie dumplings in groups of 20.
- Fill half a large saucepan with water and bring it to a rapid boil.
- Add 1 tsp salt and borax, then put in the dumplings and boil over moderately high heat for 3–4 hours. Top up with water when necessary.
- To test if the dumplings are cooked, unwrap one after 3 hours, cut into half and check if the glutinous rice is smooth to the touch. (How long you have to boil the dumplings depends on the size of the bundles of dumplings.)
- When dumplings are cooked, remove from saucepan, trim protruding leaves and tie into neat bundles of 10. Leave to hang until cool and firm for about 8–10 hours.
- To serve, unwrap dumplings and slice thinly.
- Serve with screwpine (pandan) flavoured syrup or coarsely grated young coconut and palm sugar syrup.
- To make screwpine syrup, combine desired amount of sugar, water and screwpine (pandan) leaves and boil until you get a fairly thick syrup.
- To prepare palm sugar syrup, grate desired amount of palm sugar, add water and screwpine leaves and boil for 10 minutes until syrup is fairly thick.

Note:
When using dried bamboo leaves, soak them in cold water overnight, then boil for 15 minutes. Drain.

Adding borax and salt to the boiling water prevents the leaves from sticking to the dumplings.

Pineapple–shaped Tarts

INGREDIENTS

Plain flour	560 g (1 1/4 lb)
Baking powder	2 tsp
Butter	340 g (12 oz), chilled
Castor sugar	2 Tbsp
Egg yolks	3
Vanilla essence	1 tsp
Yellow food colouring	3 drops
Salt	1/2 tsp
Boiling water	8 Tbsp
Plain flour for dusting	
Cloves	

Glaze
Egg	1
Egg yolk	1
Yellow food colouring	2 drops

METHOD

- Sift flour and baking powder together into a large mixing bowl.
- Rub butter lightly into the flour with finger tips until mixture resembles breadcrumbs.
- In a separate bowl, combine castor sugar, egg yolks, vanilla essence, yellow food colouring and salt and beat lightly in a bowl.
- Pour egg mixture into the flour. Add boiling water and mix with both hands to form a dough.
- Chill in refrigerator for 1/2 hour.

To assemble the tarts
- Divide pastry into two or three portions. Place each portion on a well-floured board or marble top. Knead until smooth. Flatten pastry with the palm of your hand and dust with flour. Roll pastry out until 0.5-cm (1/4-in) thick.
- Cut out pastry with an oval pastry cutter.
- Place a piece of pineapple filling on half of the pastry and fold the other half over it. Press the edges together with your finger and thumb. Roll the tart so that one end is tapered. Insert a clove (without pit) at the broad end to resemble a pineapple stalk.
- Using a small pair of scissors, snip rows of tiny 'v' shapes on the front half of the tart.
- In a bowl, combine the glaze ingredients.
- Place tarts on greased trays, leaving some space in between for expansion. Glaze and bake in the oven at 175°C (350°F) for 10 minutes. Reduce heat to 150°C (300°F) and continue baking for another I5–20 minutes until light brown.

Pineapple Filling

INGREDIENTS

Pineapples	5, preferably Mauritian
Coarse sugar	560 g (1 ¼ lb)
Cloves	3
Cinnamon quill	5-cm (2-in) piece
Star anise	3 segments

METHOD

- Make this a day early. Remove skin and black 'eyes' from pineapples.
- Grate pineapples coarsely (*see picture of grater on facing page*). Use a piece of muslin to squeeze out juice from pineapples but do not squeeze them too dry.
- Chop grated pineapple until fine.
- Place chopped pineapple, sugar, cloves, cinnamon quill and star anise in a heavy-bottomed saucepan.
- Cook over moderate heat for about 1 hour until almost dry. Continue cooking over low heat until mixture is thick. Stir often to prevent the pineapple from burning.
- Remove from heat and let cool. Store overnight in the refrigerator.
- Roll the pineapple into long rolls about 2.5-cm (1-in) in diameter. Cut into 1-cm (½-in) pieces. Roll each piece into a ball the size of a quail's egg.
- Place pineapple balls on a tray to chill in the refrigerator until ready for use.

Note:
Wear clean rubber gloves when grating and squeezing the pineapples.

Love Letters

INGREDIENTS

Plain flour	600 g (1 lb 5 oz), mixed with 1 Tbsp rice flour
Castor sugar	600 g (1 lb 5 oz)
Coconut	1.6 kg (3½ lb), grated
Eggs	8

METHOD

- Sun the flour and sugar separately for 2–3 hours. Sift the flour and set aside to cool.
- Using a piece of muslin, squeeze grated coconut to extract No.1 milk and set aside.
- Beat eggs and sugar in a mixing bowl.
- Place flour in another mixing bowl. Make a well in the centre and pour in a cupful of the egg mixture. Fold in the flour from the sides to form a smooth paste. Add the remaining egg mixture and gradually stir in the coconut milk.
- Pass the batter through a sieve to remove the lumps. Smooth out lumps with a little egg mixture and set aside for ½ hour.
- Heat love letter pan (*see picture on the right*) over red hot charcoal. When hot, oil both sides of the pan.
- Stir batter before using. Pour 1 Tbsp of batter onto the centre of the pan. Cover pan and place over the fire. Grill for 2–2½ minutes or until light golden. Using a knife, remove wafer from the hot pan and quickly roll into a cylindrical shape.
- Store in an airtight tin when cool. Repeat until the batter is used up.

Note:
Always sun the flour and sugar as it helps to make the love letters dry and crispy.

Beat the eggs until sugar is completely dissolved.

Make sure charcoal is red hot to give even heat. Leave more charcoal burning in another stove to replenish the grill when necessary.

Use No.2 milk to thin down the batter if it is too thick.

Do not put too much batter in the pan to avoid spillage.

After batter is poured in pan, close and tilt the pan to allow excess batter to run out on one side only.

Do not use too many pans if you do not have helpers.

Electric love letter pans are now available. Use according to manufacturer's instructions.

Lotus Seed Paste Mooncakes

INGREDIENTS

Hong Kong soft flour (high gluten flour for mooncakes)	600 g (1 lb 5 oz)
Corn oil	170 ml ($^3/_4$ cup)
Alkaline water	1 Tbsp (*recipe on page 13*)
Golden syrup	225 ml (1 cup)
Lotus seed paste	2 kg (4$^1/_2$ lb)
Melon seeds	15 g ($^1/_2$ oz)
Olive seeds	115 g ($^1/_2$ oz)
Salted egg yolks	14

Glaze

Egg	1
Egg yolk	1
Water	1 Tbsp
Golden syrup	2 tsp

METHOD

- Sift flour into a mixing bowl. Pour in corn oil and stir lightly with a fork.
- Mix the alkaline water with the golden syrup in another bowl and pour into the flour mixture. Knead into a dough and shape it into a ball. Set aside, covered, for 1 hour.
- Divide lotus seed paste into 7 equal portions.
- Combine the melon and olive seeds in a dish and divide into 7 equal portions.
- Grease both palms. Take a portion of mixed seeds and knead into a portion of lotus seed paste. Place two yolks in each portion of lotus seed paste and set aside. Repeat.
- Divide dough into 7 portions. Place each portion between plastic sheets and press to flatten, then roll out thinly. Cut each portion of dough into a large round.
- Take one dough disk and wrap it around one portion of lotus seed paste, leaving no air pockets. Roll with both hands to form a smooth round ball.
- Dust mooncake mould (*picture on this page*) with flour and knock out excess. Place the filled dough ball into the mould, pressing gently into the spaces to ensure that the cake takes up the impression from mould.
- Knock the sides of the mould gently to release cake. Repeat.
- Combine glaze ingredients in a bowl.
- Preheat oven to moderately high. Brush glaze over the top and sides of the mooncakes and bake for 10 minutes.
- Remove from oven, glaze again and bake for another 10 minutes.
- Glaze for the third time, reduce heat to low and bake for 20–30 minutes until golden brown.
- Set aside to cool. Keep for 3–5 days before serving.

Note:
Glaze cakes very lightly and evenly on top and sides. Do not allow glaze to drip around cakes. After the third glaze, remember to turn heat down low to prevent cake from cracking.

No Bake Pandan Mooncakes

INGREDIENTS

Screwpine (*pandan*) leaves	15
Koa flour (high glutinous flour for mooncakes)	455 g (1 lb)
Icing sugar	455 g (1 lb)
Salted duck's egg yolks	20–40
Water	425 ml (2 cups)
Corn oil	4 Tbsp
Rose essence	4 drops
Screwpine (*pandan*) juice	2 Tbsp
Green food colouring	A few drops
Lotus seed paste	1.5 kg (3¼ lbs)

METHOD

- Extract screwpine juice. Cut screwpine leaves finely and pound until very fine. Add 1 Tbsp water and squeeze out 2 Tbsp juice. Set aside.
- Sift flour and icing sugar together into a mixing bowl. Set aside.
- Steam salted duck's egg yolks for 10 minutes or until cooked.
- Combine water, corn oil. rose essence, food colouring and screwpine juice in a bowl. Add it to the flour mixture to form a smooth dough. Cover with a damp cloth and set aside for 2 hours before use.
- Divide lotus seed paste into 40 equal portions and roll each into a ball. Set aside.
- Remove dough to a lightly floured board and divide into 40 equal portions. Place on a tray and cover with a damp cloth to prevent drying.
- Take a piece of dough and shape it into a ball. Place it between two pieces of plastic and using a rolling pin, roll it into a thin circular sheet.
- Put one egg yolk into a portion of lotus paste and place it in the centre of the circular sheet of dough. Wrap the filling with the dough and shape it again into a ball.
- Dust mooncake mould (*picture on page 108*) with koa flour and place the filled dough in it. Press the dough into the mould to get a firm imprint, then knock the moulded dough out.
- Place it in a container to prevent cake from drying.

Note:
This version of mooncake can be kept fresh for a long time if refrigerated. Keep in an airtight container.

Birthday Longevity Buns

INGREDIENTS

Lotus seed paste   680 g (1 1/2 lb)

Dough
Self-raising flour	225 g (8 oz)
Icing sugar	3 Tbsp
Baking powder	2 tsp
Cooking oil	2 Tbsp
Vinegar	1 tsp
Milk	130 ml (2/3 cup)

METHOD

- Prepare the dough. Sift flour, icing sugar and baking powder together into a mixing bowl.
- In a separate bowl, combine cooking oil, vinegar and milk and blend.
- Add the milk mixture to the flour and stir to form a dough.
- Transfer dough to a lightly floured board and knead lightly until smooth.
- Cut dough into 2 portions and roll each into a log. Cut each into 20 pieces, then cover with a cloth to prevent them from drying out.
- Roll lotus seed paste and cut into 40 pieces. Roll each piece into a ball and set aside.
- Take a piece of dough and shape into a small cup. Place a ball of lotus seed paste in the centre of the dough and mould it into the shape of a small peach. Use the back of a kitchen knife to make an impression along the centre to resemble a peach.
- Repeat with the remaining dough and lotus seed paste. Put a piece of greaseproof paper under each bun. Rub a little red food colouring at the tip of each bun and steam all over rapidly boiling water for 6–8 minutes.
- To serve: Stack buns in a pyramid on a round plate. Serve hot or cold.

Note:
Use a steamer with a tight fitting lid to prevent steam from escaping. This ensures a light textured bun.

auspiciousbanquets

FESTIVE COOKING – THE BEST OF SINGAPORE'S RECIPES

Crabs in Tomato and Curry

INGREDIENTS

Flower crab	1.2 kg (2 lb 11 oz)
Cooking oil	6 Tbsp
Shallots	55 g (2 oz), peeled and finely sliced
Ginger	$1/2$ Tbsp, peeled and finely sliced
Garlic	2 cloves, peeled and finely sliced
Tomatoes	2, cut into wedges
Tomato ketchup	6 Tbsp
Curry powder	2 Tbsp
Sugar	4 tsp
Salt	1 tsp
Water	340 ml (1$1/2$ cups)
Evaporated milk	6 Tbsp

METHOD

- Clean and cut crabs into quarters. Break claws gently.
- Add cooking oil to a heated wok and fry shallots, ginger and garlic until fragrant. Add tomatoes and tomato ketchup and fry until oil bubbles through.
- Add curry powder and stir, then add sugar, salt and water and bring to the boil.
- Put crabs in, stir well and cook, covered, over moderate heat for 15 minutes. (If crab is still not cooked, continue boiling with the lid off, until done.)
- Add evaporated milk, stir and heat through. Transfer to a large serving plate and serve.

Fried Crabs with Spicy Sichuan Yellow Bean Paste

INGREDIENTS

Crabs	3, approximately 1.8 kg (4 lb)
Shallots	8, peeled
Garlic	4 cloves, peeled
Red chillies	2, seeded
Ginger	4 slices, peeled
Lard or cooking oil	4 Tbsp
Spicy Sichuan yellow bean paste	2 Tbsp (*see recipe below*)
Egg	1, lightly beaten
Spring onions	3, cut into 3-cm (1¹/₂-in) lengths
Lard	2 Tbsp

Gravy

Water	225 ml (1 cup)
Sugar	1 Tbsp
Vinegar	1 tsp
MSG	1 tsp, optional
Salt	¹/₄ tsp
Soy sauce	2 tsp

METHOD

- Shell crabs and scrub them clean. Cut into 4 pieces, separate the claws and crack them lightly.
- Combine shallots, garlic, chillies and ginger and pound to a paste.
- Heat a pan, add lard or cooking oil and fry shallot mixture until fragrant. Add the yellow bean paste and stir, then pour in the gravy ingredients and bring to the boil.
- Add the crabs, stir and cover the pan. Cook for 10–15 minutes or until the crabs are done.
- Add more water if too dry, then pour in the beaten egg, spring onions and lard.
- Stir to combine and heat through, then transfer to a serving dish. Serve hot.

Spicy Sichuan Yellow Bean Paste

INGREDIENTS

Yellow bean paste (*taucheo*)	115 g (¹/₂ cup)
Plum paste	2 Tbsp
Hot chilli sauce	4 Tbsp
Sesame oil	2 tsp

METHOD

- Blend together all the ingredients. Store in the refrigerator.

Baked Crabs

INGREDIENTS

Crabs	8, medium-sized, whole
Eggs	2
Minced pork	225 g (8 oz)
Prawns	225 g (8 oz), shelled, deveined and finely chopped
Breadcrumbs	2 Tbsp, soaked in 2 Tbsp water
Plain flour for dusting	
Breadcrumbs	

Seasoning

Salt	1 tsp
MSG	1 tsp, optional
Pepper	$1/2$ tsp
Lard	2 Tbsp
Dark soy sauce	1 tsp
Soy sauce	1 tsp

METHOD

- Steam whole crabs over rapidly boiling water for 20 minutes. Do not remove lid while steaming. When cooked, remove from the steamer and leave to cool.
- Pick out the crabmeat and set aside. Reserve the shells for stuffing.
- In a bowl, combine seasoning ingredients together with 1 egg.
- Add minced pork, prawns, soaked breadcrumbs and crabmeat and mix lightly.
- Dust crab shells with flour. Fill the shells with the crabmeat mixture and grill or bake in a pre-heated oven at 190°C (375°F) until cooked, about 30–45 minutes.
- Beat the remaining egg. Remove baked crabs from the oven and brush with the egg. Sprinkle on the breadcrumbs and return crabs to the oven for another 5–7 minutes. Serve crabs garnished with coriander leaves.

Fried Prawns in Salt

INGREDIENTS

Lard or cooking oil	4 Tbsp
Prawns	600 g (1 lb 5 oz), washed and trimmed
Water	4 Tbsp
Salt	2 tsp

METHOD

• Heat a wok until very hot, and add 3 Tbsp lard or cooking oil. When oil is smoking hot, add the prawns, sprinkle with water and stir. Cover the wok and let prawns cook over high heat for 3 minutes.

• Remove prawns and drain. Clean the wok and heat the wok until it is very hot. Return prawns to the wok, add the salt and the remaining 1 Tbsp of lard or cooking oil, and toss prawns until evenly coated with salt.

• Cook for $1/2$ minute and serve immediately.

Note:
Lard is preferable to cooking oil as it can take intense heat and not burn.

Shark's Fin Soup

INGREDIENTS

Chicken	900 g (2 lb), quartered
Water	1.4 litres (5^1/$_2$ cups)
Peppercorns	1 tsp
Oyster sauce	1 Tbsp
Soy sauce	1 Tbsp
MSG	1 tsp, optional
Sherry or wine	1 tsp
Pepper	To taste
Crabmeat	225 g (8 oz), steamed
Prepared shark's fin	115 g (4 oz)
Eggs	2, beaten with 2 Tbsp water
Cornflour	5 Tbsp
Water	55 ml (^{1}/$_4$ cup)
Lard	2 Tbsp

METHOD

- Place chicken, water and peppercorns into a stock pot and bring to the boil. Let it simmer for 1−1^1/$_2$ hours until the stock is reduced to two-thirds. Strain into another saucepan, and return chicken stock to the boil.
- Stir the oyster sauce, soy sauce, MSG, if using, sherry or wine and pepper into the stock. Add crabmeat and shark's fin and bring to the boil again. Stir in the beaten eggs.
- In a bowl, combine cornflour and 55 ml (^{1}/$_4$ cup) water and stir to blend. Stir it gradually into the soup. Lastly, stir in the lard. Serve hot.

Note:
Prepared shark's fin is available at certain supermarkets.

Stir-fried Frog's Legs

INGREDIENTS

Frog's legs	455 g (1 lb)
Cooking oil	285 ml (1 1/4 cups)
Lard or cooking oil	4 Tbsp
Young ginger	1/2 Tbsp, peeled and thinly sliced
Garlic	2 cloves, peeled and chopped
Carrot	1/2, skinned, boiled and thinly sliced
Tapioca flour or cornflour	1 1/2 tsp, mixed with 2 Tbsp water
Spring onions	3, cut into 4-cm (1 1/2-in) lengths

Marinade

Salt	1/2 tsp
Sugar	1/2 tsp
MSG	1/2 tsp, optional
Cooking oil	1 Tbsp
Pepper	A dash

Seasoning

Salt	1/2 tsp
MSG	1 tsp, optional
Sugar	1 tsp
Sherry or brandy	1 tsp
Sesame oil	1/2 tsp
Chicken stock	4 Tbsp, or 1/2 chicken stock cube with 4 Tbsp water

METHOD

- Wash frog's legs. Rub all over with marinade ingredients and set aside for 10 minutes.
- Combine all the seasoning ingredients in a bowl and set aside for later use.
- In a wok, heat cooking oil until smoking hot. Put in half the frog's legs and fry for 2 minutes. Remove. Reheat oil and fry the remaining legs.
- In a clean wok, heat 2 Tbsp of the lard or cooking oil. Stir-fry the ginger, garlic and carrots for 1/2 minute. Add seasoning ingredients and frog's legs and stir-fry for another 1/2 minute.
- Pour in the flour solution and stir until the sauce is sufficiently thick.
- Add the spring onions and remaining lard or cooking oil. Stir and transfer to a plate. Serve hot.

Rendang Ikan

FISH IN RICH COCONUT GRAVY

INGREDIENTS

Spotted Spanish Mackerel (*ikan tenggiri papan*)	455 g (1 lb), cut into pieces
Coconut	455 g (1 lb), grated
Water	225 ml (1 cup)
Cooking oil	4 Tbsp
Curry powder	2 tsp
Tamarind pulp (*asam*)	1 Tbsp, mixed with 113 ml (¹/₂ cup) water, strained
Dried sour fruit (*asam gelugur*)	1 slice

Marinade

Sugar	1 tsp
Salt	³/₄ tsp
Tamarind pulp (*asam*)	1 Tbsp, mixed with 2 Tbsp water and strained

Rempah

Shallots	113 g (4 oz), peeled
Lemon grass	1 stalk
Galangal	¹/₂ Tbsp, peeled
Red chillies	6, seeded
Ginger	4 slices, peeled
Shrimp paste (*belacan*)	1 tsp
Garlic	1 clove, peeled
Turmeric	¹/₂ Tbsp, peeled, or ¹/₂ tsp ground turmeric
Kaffir lime leaves (*daun limau purut*)	4

Seasoning

Dried sour fruit (*asam gelugur*)	1 slice
Sugar	2 tsp
Salt	1 tsp
MSG	1 tsp, optional

METHOD

- Rub marinade ingredients all over fish and leave to marinate for 20 minutes.
- Combine *rempah* ingredients and pound to a fine paste. Set aside.
- Place grated coconut in a piece of muslin and squeeze to extract No.1 milk. Set aside. Add water to the grated coconut and squeeze again to extract No. 2 milk. Collect in a separate bowl and set aside.
- Heat a wok until hot. Heat 4 Tbsp cooking oil and fry curry powder and *rempah* paste over moderate heat until oil bubbles through. Add 3 Tbsp No.1 milk, a spoonful at a time, and continue frying until the paste is oily and fragrant.
- Now add in No.2 milk and tamarind juice and bring to the boil. Add dried sour fruit slice, seasoning ingredients, marinated fish and continue to cook over moderate heat for 7–8 minutes.
- Reduce heat to low. Stir in the remaining No.1 milk and simmer for 5 minutes uncovered.
- Remove from heat and serve hot.

festivefillers

FESTIVE COOKING – THE BEST OF SINGAPORE'S RECIPES

Nasi Minyak

GHEE RICE MALAY STYLE

INGREDIENTS

Water	800 ml (3^1/$_2$ cups)
Milk	170 ml (^{3}/$_4$ cup)
Salt	1^1/$_2$ tsp
Rose essence	4 drops
Ghee	140 g (5 oz)
Cardamom	15, lightly crushed
Cinnamon quill	7-cm (2^3/$_4$-in) piece
Cloves	6
Shallots	5, or 1 small onion, peeled and thinly sliced
Ginger	1 Tbsp, peeled and chopped
Garlic	1 tsp, peeled and chopped
Rice	625 g (1 lb 6 oz), washed and drained
Crisp-fried shallots	2 Tbsp (recipe on page 12)
Sultanas	115 g (4 oz), fried in a little cooking oil, drained
Sliced almonds	55 g (2 oz), lightly toasted

METHOD

- Combine water, milk, salt and rose essence in a saucepan and bring to the boil.
- Heat ghee in a wok and fry cardamom, cinnamon quill and cloves for a minute. Add shallots, ginger and garlic. Stir-fry until shallots turn light brown.
- Add rice to the wok and stir until it absorbs the ghee.
- Pour in the boiling milk mixture and stir to blend. Then transfer rice to cook in an electric rice cooker until done.
- Fluff rice up to separate grains and remove from heat.
- To serve: Place rice on a large serving plate and garnish with crisp-fried shallots, sultanas and almonds.

Note:
Rice can be kept warm by steaming over low heat in a saucepan.

Pressed Rice

INGREDIENTS

Rice	620 g (1 lb 5 oz), washed
Water	1.2 litres (5^1/$_3$ cups)
Salt	^{1}/$_2$ tsp
Screwpine (*pandan*) leaves	4, knotted

METHOD

- Soak rice for 4 hours or overnight.
- Drain rice and place in a heavy-bottomed saucepan.
- Pour in water and salt and bring to the boil over moderate heat. Stir 2–3 times.
- When steam holes appear, do not touch the rice anymore.
- Reduce the heat to low and allow rice to cook for 45 minutes.
- Stir and mash rice with a wooden spoon and continue cooking for another ^{1}/$_2$ hour or until rice is very dry.
- Wet a square piece of white muslin and scoop the rice into it. Gather the edges of the muslin and tie it with a string.
- With the rice in the bag, pound the rice into a smooth paste and press it flat.
- Place the knotted screwpine leaves into the rice bag. Place a wooden chopping board or a heavy object on top of the bag of rice to compress the rice paste. Leave overnight.
- To serve: Remove rice from the bag, slice thinly and serve.

Jakarta Nasi Lemak Kuning

YELLOW COCONUT RICE JAKARTA STYLE

INGREDIENTS

Coconut	455 g (1 lb), grated
Water for the coconut milk	
Cooking oil	2 Tbsp
Cinnamon quill	5-cm (2-in) piece
Shallots	30 g (1 oz), peeled and thinly sliced
Garlic	2 cloves, peeled
Lemon grass	2 stalks, crushed
Fragrant Thai rice	570 g (1 1/4 lb), washed and drained
Salt	1 1/2 level Tbsp
Chicken stock cube	1, crushed
Ground turmeric	1/2 tsp
Lemon or lime juice	1 Tbsp
Screwpine (*pandan*) leaves	4, knotted
Crisp-fried shallots	4 Tbsp (*recipe on page 12*)

METHOD

- Place grated coconut in a piece of muslin and squeeze to extract No.1 milk. Add some water to the grated coconut and squeeze again for No.2 milk. Combine No.1 and No. 2 milk in a saucepan and add enough water to make a total volume of 680 ml (3 cups).
- Heat coconut milk until scalding hot.
- In another pan, heat the cooking oil and fry cinnamon quill, shallots, garlic and lemon grass until light brown. Add rice, stir for 2 minutes, then add salt, chicken stock cube, ground turmeric and lemon or lime juice. Toss for 2 minutes.
- Pour in one-third of the coconut milk and stir over low heat until milk is absorbed into the rice.
- Transfer rice into an electric rice cooker. Pour in the rest of the coconut milk, add screwpine leaves and cook until rice is done.
- Fluff rice up with a fork, discard screwpine leaves and serve, garnished with crisp-fried shallots.

Note:
Thinly sliced, seeded chilli can also be used as garnish.

Crispy Noodles with Prawns

INGREDIENTS

Prawns	600 g (1 lb 5 oz), large
MSG	$1/4$ tsp, optional
Ginger	1 tsp, peeled and pounded
Cooking oil for deep-frying	
Lard	4 Tbsp
Ginger	6 slices, peeled
Garlic	1 tsp, peeled and pounded
Dried mushrooms	4, soaked and sliced
Chinese flowering cabbage (*choy sum*)	280 g (10 oz), cut into 3-cm ($1^1/2$-in) lengths
Chicken stock	455 ml (2 cups)

Thickening

Cornflour	2 Tbsp
Water	4 Tbsp

Seasoning

Soy sauce	1 Tbsp
Oyster sauce	1 Tbsp
Sugar	$1/2$ tsp
MSG	1 tsp
Salt	$1/4$ tsp
Sesame oil	$1/2$ tsp

Noodles

Water	560 ml ($2^1/2$ cups)
Chicken stock cube	1
Cooking oil	2 Tbsp
Egg noodles	200 g (7 oz), dried

METHOD

- Shell prawns, devein and marinate with MSG, if using, and ginger.
- Prepare the thickening solution. Combine cornflour and water in a bowl and set aside.
- In another bowl, combine seasoning ingredients and set aside.
- To prepare noodles: Bring 560 ml ($2^1/2$ cups) of water to the boil with chicken stock cube and cooking oil. Add noodles and cook until noodles soften for about 3–4 minutes. Plunge into cold water and drain. Set aside to cool for $1/2$ hour.
- Heat wok until very hot, then pour in cooking oil for deep-frying. When oil is very hot, add in the noodles in batches and fry until light brown and crispy.
- Using a wire ladle, transfer noodles onto absorbent paper. Keep the noodles warm.
- Heat a clean wok until very hot. Add 3 Tbsp lard and fry ginger and garlic until light brown. Add the mushrooms and flowering cabbage stalks and stir-fry briefly. Add the flowering cabbage leaves, chicken stock and seasoning and bring to the boil.
- Add the marinated prawns, cover pan and cook over high heat for 2 minutes.
- Gradually stir in the thickening solution. Lower heat, let sauce come to the boil again and add the last 1 Tbsp lard.
- Transfer noodles to a serving plate. Pour sauce over the crispy noodles. Serve at once.

Thai Pineapple Rice

INGREDIENTS

Cooking oil	3 Tbsp
Dried prawns	55 g (2 oz), coarsely pounded
Ham	55 g (2 oz), diced
Pineapple	225 g (8 oz), diced
Butter	2 Tbsp
Shallots or onions	55 g (2 oz), peeled and finely sliced
Garlic	2 cloves, peeled and finely sliced
Cinnamon quill	2-cm (1-in) piece
Fragrant Thai rice	570 g (1 1/4 lb), washed and drained
Pineapple juice	170 ml (3/4 cup)
Screwpine (*pandan*) leaves	4, knotted
Water	800 ml (3 1/2 cups), boiling

Seasoning

Curry powder	1 tsp
Ground turmeric	1/2 tsp
Chicken stock cube	1, crushed
Salt	2 tsp
Lemon juice	1 Tbsp

METHOD

- Heat a wok until very hot. Add cooking oil and when hot, fry the dried prawns and ham until brown. Transfer to a plate and set aside.
- In the same wok, fry the pineapple cubes for 5 minutes until light brown. Set aside.
- Add butter to the wok and fry shallots or onions, garlic and cinnamon quill until light brown. Stir in seasoning ingredients, then add the rice. Toss until the oil is absorbed. Stir in pineapple juice.
- Transfer into an electric rice cooker, add screwpine leaves and 800 ml (3 1/2 cups) boiling water and cook.
- When rice is done, leave aside for about 1/2 hour to dry. Fluff with a fork and serve hot.

sweettreats

FESTIVE COOKING – THE BEST OF SINGAPORE'S RECIPES

Sar-sargon

CRISPY RICE AND COCONUT CANDY

INGREDIENTS

No.1 Thai rice	600 g (1 lb 5 oz), washed and soaked overnight
Coconut	3, grated
Salt	$1/2$ tsp
Lime paste	$1/4$ tsp
Eggs	2, lightly beaten
Sugar	225–340 g (8–12 oz)

METHOD

- Drain rice, spread it on a tray and leave in the sun until it is very dry.
- Grind rice until fine and set aside.
- Place grated coconut in a large bowl and rub salt and lime paste into it. Add the eggs and mix lightly.
- Add the rice flour a little at a time and lightly rub it into the coconut mixture.
- In a heated wok, fry the coconut mixture (without cooking oil) until dry and brittle. Stir often to prevent it getting burnt.
- When mixture becomes grainy and free from lumps, reduce heat and stir until it becomes crispy.
- Add the sugar, stir for 2 minutes and remove from heat. Leave to cool in the wok. Taste a spoonful for desired sweetness and add sugar, if necessary.

Note:
A brass or bronze wok is ideal for this recipe as it allows the sar-sargon to remain pale and off-white in colour, while becoming brittle and crispy at the same time. However, an iron or thick aluminium wok can be used as well.

As far as possible, use a charcoal fire for this recipe for best results.

The lime paste used must be very smooth and pasty to mix well with the coconut.

Ready packed ground rice can be substituted for the No. 1 Thai rice.

Kuih Lapis Batavia

INDONESIAN LAYER CAKE

INGREDIENTS

Butter	455 g (1 lb)
Mixed spice	1 tsp (*see recipe below*)
Plain flour	115 g (4 oz)
Egg yolks	17
Sugar	255 g (9 oz)
Egg whites	5
Brandy	2 Tbsp

METHOD

- In a bowl, beat butter until creamy. Set aside.
- Sift mixed spice and flour together into another bowl. Set aside.
- Place eggs yolks and 200 g (7 oz) of the sugar in a bowl and beat until thick. Set aside.
- Place the remaining sugar in another bowl with the egg whites and beat until thick.
- Alternately fold in the egg yolk mixture and the egg white mixture into the creamed butter. Add a little flour each time until all is blended. Lastly, add the brandy.

- Grease the bottom and sides of a baking pan with butter.
- Cut a piece of greaseproof paper to snugly fit the base of the pan. Place the paper in the pan and grease with butter.
- Heat the pan under a moderately hot grill for a minute. Remove it and pour one ladleful of cake batter into the pan, allowing it to spread evenly over the base of the pan.
- Bake for 5 minutes or until light brown, then remove the pan from the grill. Prick the top of the cake using a skewer to prevent air bubbles from forming.
- Pour another ladleful of cake batter over the cooked layer and bake again. Repeat the process as for the first layer, until all the batter is used up.
- When done, tip the cake out of the pan at once, and let it cool for 1/2 hour.

Mixed Spice

INGREDIENTS

Cinnamon quill	30 g (1 oz)
Cloves	20
Star anise	1
Green cardamom	20

METHOD

- Wash the cinnamon quill, cloves and star anise, then let them dry thoroughly in the sun.
- Remove the stems from the cloves.
- Place them in a saucepan and toast over low heat for 20 minutes.
- Remove the husk from the cardamom to extract the seeds.
- Pound all the spices together until very fine, then pass it through a fine sieve. Store in a clean dry bottle for future use.

Moscovis

THIRTEEN-LAYER FRUIT CAKE JAKARTA STYLE

INGREDIENTS

Egg yolks	22
Icing sugar	300 g (11 oz)
Butter	500 g (1 lb 2 oz)
Egg whites	8
Sugar	1 tsp
Plain flour	200 g (7 oz)
Condensed milk	4 Tbsp
Rum	1 Tbsp
Vanilla essence	1 tsp
Orange peel	2 Tbsp, chopped
Raisins	2 Tbsp
Almonds	2 Tbsp, chopped
Cherries	2 Tbsp, sliced

METHOD

- Put egg yolks and icing sugar in a bowl and beat until creamy.
- In another bowl, beat butter until creamy.
- In a separate bowl, beat egg whites with 1 tsp sugar until thick.
- Mix egg yolk mixture and butter, add flour, egg white mixture, condensed milk, rum and vanilla essence. Stir gently to blend.
- Pour a layer of the cake batter into a greased cake pan, and sprinkle with some of the raisins, orange peel and almonds. Bake under a grill at moderate heat for 4–5 minutes. Pour another layer of batter over the baked layer, sprinkle with raisins, orange peel and almonds and bake again. Repeat this until you get a 13-layered cake.
- Before baking the final layer, decorate with sliced almonds and cherries.
- Place cake on a rack (*picture on the left*) and let stand for 10 minutes before turning over onto a plate.

Kuih Sarlat

GLUTINOUS RICE CAKE WITH CUSTARD TOPPING

INGREDIENTS

Coconut Milk
Coconut	1.6 kg (3^1/$_2$ lb), grated
Salt	1^1/$_2$ tsp
Castor sugar	1 Tbsp

Custard Topping
Plain flour	1 Tbsp
Cornflour	1 Tbsp
No.1 coconut milk	455 ml (2 cups)
Screwpine (*pandan*) leaves	10, pounded to a fine pulp
Coarse sugar	370 g (13 oz)
Eggs	10, lightly beaten
Green food colouring	1 tsp

Glutinous Rice
Glutinous rice	625 g (1 lb 6 oz), washed and soaked overnight
Screwpine (*pandan*) leaves	6, knotted
No.1 coconut milk	170 ml (^{3}/$_4$ cup)
No.2 coconut milk	225 ml (1 cup)

METHOD

For the coconut milk
- Place grated coconut in piece of muslin and squeeze to extract about 625 ml (2^3/$_4$ cups) No.1 milk. Set aside 455 ml (2 cups) for the custard topping.
- Pour the remaining 170 ml (^{3}/$_4$ cup) No.1 milk into a separate jug for the glutinous rice. Add salt and castor sugar to this portion of the milk and stir until dissolved. Set aside.
- Now pour 340 ml (1^1/$_2$ cups) water to the grated coconut and using the piece of muslin, squeeze again for No.2 milk. Set aside 225 ml (1 cup) of the No.2 milk.

For the custard topping
- Combine plain flour, cornflour and 4 Tbsp from 455 ml (2 cups) of the No.1 coconut milk and mix until smooth.
- Add the remaining milk to the pounded screwpine leaves. Mix and strain through a fine muslin.
- Blend the milk with the flour mixture and set aside.

- Place coarse sugar and beaten eggs in a heavy-bottomed saucepan over a very low heat. Stir constantly until sugar dissolves.
- Remove from the heat and add the flour mixture and green food colouring. Stir and set aside.

For the glutinous rice
- Drain glutinous rice and steam with screwpine leaves over rapidly boiling water for 15 minutes. (Before steaming, make steam holes in glutinous rice using the handle of wooden spoon.)
- Transfer glutinous rice to a saucepan, pour in the No.2 coconut milk and mix. Leave covered, for 5 minutes.
- Return glutinous rice to the steamer. Steam for another 7 minutes. Transfer to a saucepan and mix in salted No.1 milk. Steam again for another 5 minutes.
- Transfer glutinous rice to a round pan, 30-cm (12-in) in diameter and 5-cm (2-in) deep. Press rice down firmly with a banana leaf or a thick piece of soft plastic.

To assemble kuih sarlat
- Steam the pan of glutinous rice over boiling water for 15 minutes.
- Re-heat the custard topping for 2 minutes, stirring often. Pour it over the glutinous rice, cover and steam over moderately high heat for 15 minutes or until it changes colour and sets, forming slight ridges on the surface.
- Reduce heat to very low and continue steaming for 45 minutes, or until a knife comes out clean when inserted into the centre of the custard layer.
- Transfer tray to a wire rack to cool completely before cutting.

Note:
Remember to make steam holes in the glutinous rice before you steam the rice each time.

While steaming, wipe the water droplets on the underside of the wok's lid from time to time as they can discolour the cake.

Replenish wok with boiling water when necessary during steaming.

Kembang Goyang

ROSE-SHAPED FRITTERS

INGREDIENTS

Eggs	5
Sugar	225 g (8 oz)
Plain flour	285 g (9 oz), sifted
Water	240 ml (1 cup and 1 Tbsp)

Cooking oil for deep-frying

METHOD

- Beat eggs and sugar together. Set aside.
- Put flour into a large bowl and make a well in the centre. Gradually pour in half of the egg mixture, blending flour from side of bowl to mix.
- Add remaining egg mixture and water gradually, and blend until batter is smooth.
- Strain batter and let it stand for $1/2$ hour before frying.
- To fry the batter: Heat cooking oil in a wok, then hold the rose-patterned mould (*see picture on the left*) in the oil to heat.
- Dip the heated mould in the batter until the batter almost reaches the top of the mould. (Do not immerse the mould completely in the batter, though.) Hold it in the batter for a moment, then dip the mould with the batter coating it, into the oil.
- Move the mould about in the oil until batter changes colour and the fritter falls away from the mould. Cook until fritter turns a light golden brown.
- Transfer the fritter onto absorbent paper. Fry remaining batter and cool fritters before storing in an airtight container.

Limpot Durian

DURIAN CAKE

INGREDIENTS

Durian pulp	680 g (1¹/₂ lb)
Coarse sugar	55 g (2 oz), for caramel
Coarse sugar	340 g (12 oz)

METHOD

- Place durian pulp in a food processor and blend to form a smooth paste.
- Heat the 55 g (2 oz) sugar in a non-stick wok until it caramelizes and becomes dark brown.
- Remove from heat, add the durian pulp and the 340 g (12 oz) sugar. Stir.
- Cook over moderate heat until paste becomes firm. Stir often to prevent paste from burning. Reduce heat, stir until paste is very dry and stiff. Remove from heat to cool.
- Divide durian paste into 4 or 5 parts whilst warm. Shape each part into a smooth thick roll. Wrap the rolls in thick plastic or cellophane paper. Use thread or a thin cord to tie both ends.
- Cut up rolls into smaller pieces to serve.

Au Nee

SWEET YAM PASTE

INGREDIENTS

Gingko nuts	115 g (4 oz), washed and shelled
Sugar	225 g (8 oz)
Water	4 Tbsp
Pumpkin	225 g (8 oz), skinned and cubed
Yam	900 g (2 lb), skinned and sliced
Lard	6 Tbsp
Castor sugar	12 Tbsp
Shallots	3, peeled and thinly sliced

METHOD

- In a small saucepan, place gingko nuts, half the sugar and 2 Tbsp water and bring to the boil over low heat for 45 minutes until sugar is absorbed into the nuts. Add more water a little at a time while cooking to prevent the sugar from burning.
- Set aside to cool, then halve gingko nuts, removing centre fibre if any.
- In a heavy-bottomed saucepan, combine pumpkin, the remaining sugar and 2 Tbsp water and boil over low heat until the sugar is absorbed. As before, add more water a little at a time while cooking to prevent sugar from burning. Set pumpkin aside.
- Steam yam slices over rapidly boiling water until very soft.
- Place half of the yam in a food processor with 2 Tbsp lard and half of the castor sugar. Blend to a smooth paste. Transfer to a bowl and repeat with the remaining yam, 2 Tbsp lard and castor sugar.
- Heat the final 2 Tbsp lard in a wok and fry the sliced shallots until light brown. Add in the yam paste and stir-fry over low heat for $1/2$ minute.
- Transfer to a shallow serving bowl.
- Place pumpkin cubes around sides of the bowl and gingko nuts on the yam paste. Serve hot.

Sweet Almond Creme

INGREDIENTS

Almonds	285 g (10 oz)
Water	855 ml (4 cups), boiling
Sugar	285 g (10 oz), boiled in 115 ml (1/2 cup) water until dissolved
Almond essence	2 drops, optional

Thickening

Rice flour	3–4 Tbsp
Water	170 ml (3/4 cup)
Milk	170 ml (3/4 cup)

METHOD

- Scald almonds with boiling water and drain. Blend until very fine, using some of the measured water. Strain through a fine sieve into a saucepan. Blend remaining almond bits and sieve again. Add the remaining water and set aside.
- Combine thickening ingredients in a bowl and mix to a fine paste.
- Bring the blended almonds to the boil over moderate heat, stirring until it boils. Add the sugar syrup and stir in the flour paste.
- Reduce heat but keep boiling for 5 minutes until the almond mixture thickens. Remove pan from the heat and add in the almond essence, if using.
- Serve hot.

Sweet Red Bean and Lotus Seed Soup

INGREDIENTS

Red beans	260 g (9 oz)
Water	570 ml (2^1/$_2$ cups) + 1.7 litres (7^1/$_2$ cups) + 1 litre (4^1/$_2$ cups)
Dried orange peel	^{1}/$_2$ piece, thinly sliced
Screwpine (*pandan*) leaves	4, knotted
Sugar	225 g (8 oz)
Lotus seeds in syrup	1 can

METHOD

- Bring red beans and the 570 ml (2^1/$_2$ cups) water to a rapid boil for ^{1}/$_2$ hour. Drain and rinse with cold water.
- Put the cooked beans and the 1.7 litres (7^1/$_2$ cups) water into a pressure cooker and boil for 45 minutes. Leave beans in cooker for ^{1}/$_2$ hour to release pressure.
- Now pour in another 1 litre (4^1/$_2$ cups) water and add in the dried orange peel and screwpine leaves. Bring to the boil, stirring until beans are blended into the liquid.
- Reduce heat. Boil gently until soup thickens; add sugar and lotus seeds with syrup and continue boiling for 45 minutes.
- Stir occasionally to prevent the beans from sticking to the bottom of the cooker. Serve hot.

glossaryofingredients

FESTIVE COOKING – THE BEST OF SINGAPORE'S RECIPES

SPICES ● ● ● ● ○ ○

1. Aniseed
Similar in flavour as star anise, aniseed is popular in Chinese cooking, adding a delicate licorice taste to sweet and savoury dishes. It is available whole, as tiny egg-shaped seeds, or in powdered form and can be bought in health food stores, Chinese delicatessens and some large supermarkets. It is also used in baking, especially biscuits and cakes, in preserving, such as plums and gherkins, in anise-flavoured liqueurs and drinks, and to mask the strong flavours of some cough medicines.

2. Cardamom
Cardamom is the world's most expensive spice after saffron. Cardamom pods are the dried fruits of a perennial plant of the ginger family indigenous to Sri Lanka and south India. The pale green oval pods, which are the best variety, contain 15–20 brown or black seeds. The white pods are simply green pods that have been bleached in the sun.

3, 4, 5. Chilli
Native to Mexico, chillies are now available in many forms – fresh, dried, powdered, flaked as well in the form of sauces, *sambal* and pastes. They range from mild to wild, and the smaller the chilli, the hotter it is, e.g. bird's eye chillies.

Chillies are used either unripe, when they are green, or ripe, after they turn red. Ripe chillies are hotter than green ones. Red chillies are usually pounded or ground into a paste, chopped or used whole for flavouring, or cut in different ways for garnishing. Green chillies are generally used whole for flavouring, or cut in different ways, for garnishing. Both red and green chillies are also available pickled. Dried chillies are pounded or ground and used for flavouring and seasoning.

Related to cayenne and Tabasco chillies, the colour of bird's eye chillies may range from deep red to cream, yellow or orange. Thin-fleshed with a deep fiery heat, its flavour may range from mild to sweet.

6. Cinnamon
Cinnamon, the edible bark of the tree native to Sri Lanka, is probably the most popular cooking spice in the Western world. The innermost layer of the bark is sold as thin, fragile quills in India, Sri Lanka, Indonesia and Malaysia and Singapore and is used for flavouring meat, poultry and desserts. The spice is also available powdered, but its flavour and aroma dissipate rather quickly in this form.

7. Clove
Cloves are actually the flower buds of a tree of the myrtle family indigenous to the Maluku Island (Moluccas) or the Spice Islands. The buds are harvested and dried under the sun for days. Cloves have a stronger flavour than most other spices and are therefore used in smaller quantities.

8. Coriander seeds
With their clean, lemony flavour, coriander seeds are a major component of most curry powder used in India, Sri Lanka, Indonesia, Malaysia and other countries. Freshly ground coriander is more fragrant than coriander that is purchased already powdered.

9. Cumin
Cumin is used in Middle Eastern, Asian and Mediterranean cooking. This aromatic spice has a nutty flavour and is available whole or ground. It is popularly used to flavour curries, stews and Indian yoghurt drinks (*lassi*).

10. Fenugreek
The seeds and tender sprouted leaves of fenugreek, native to Europe and Asia, are both edible. The seeds, with their bitter flavour, are an important component of Indian curry powders. The seeds are also used whole in some Sri Lankan and Malaysian dishes, particularly seafood curries.

11. Five-spice powder
Frequently used in all sorts of Chinese dishes, it summons up the taste and smell of China. As the name implies, it is made up of five ground spices – Szechuan pepper, cinnamon, clove, fennel seeds and star anise.

Available from delicatessens, Chinese markets and some health food shops, it should be kept in a sealed container in a dry place. Like most spices, it will keep for several months but will gradually lose its fragrance and flavour and therefore should not be kept for too long.

12. Galangal
Greater galangal is native to Malaysia and Java. It has a delicate flavour and is used fresh in Malaysian, Indonesian and Thai cooking. When the fresh variety is not available, dried and powdered galangal can be used instead.

The young rhizome is pale pink and is more tender and flavourful than the mature one, which is beige in colour. Galangal belongs to the ginger family but cannot be used as a substitute for the common ginger, as its pungency and tang is distinctively different. It is added to curries or dishes in slices, chunks or as a paste. As it is quite fibrous, chop it into small pieces before pounding or grinding it.

13. Garlic
Garlic is used with almost anything, except maybe dessert. Its flavour depends on how it is prepared – cooked garlic being much milder than raw, chopped garlic. It can be used raw or fried, poached, roasted or sautéed, and can be cooked peeled or unpeeled. Choose a firm, hard head of garlic with no soft or discoloured patches. Do not refrigerate but store in a cool, dry place.

14. Ginger
Ginger, a fleshy rhizome, is used in the West to make gingerbread, ginger beer, candied ginger and chocolate ginger. Fresh ginger is a basic ingredient in many Asian cuisines. It is usually sliced, finely chopped, pounded or ground and used in savoury dishes. Sometimes the juice is extracted and used.

15. Nutmeg
Buy whole and grate as needed. Nutmeg is used to flavour soups, vegetables, breads and cakes. A true Bolognese sauce is not complete without grated nutmeg.

16. Onion
Onions are indispensable in our day-to-day cooking. There are dry onions and green onions. Dry onions are left in the ground to mature and have a tougher, outer skin for longer storage. Green onions are merely young and immature. There are many varieties and many ways to use them.

17. Oom (ajowan) seeds
Also called omum seed, carom seed or Bishop's weed, this is the small seed of a herb belonging to the cumin and parsley family, and has the flavour of thyme. It is used sparingly in Indian lentil dishes and pickles due to its strong flavour.

18, 19. Pepper
Peppers are small, round berries that grow in trailing clusters. They start off a deep green and turn red as they ripen. Black pepper is obtained by drying the green berries in the sun, which makes the outer skin black and shrivelled.

White pepper is obtained by packing the ripe berries in sacks, soaking them in slow-flowing water for eight days and then rubbing off the softened outer skin. The inner portion is then dried in the sun for several days until it turns a creamy white. White pepper is hotter than black pepper, but it is not as fragrant.

20. Shallot
A small bulb with a sweeter, lighter, more delicate flavour than an onion. There are a number of varieties including grey, pink and brown. Most easily obtained in spring and summer, shallots are often required in dishes from France.

21. Star anise
Star anise comes from a tree belonging to the magnolia family. The dried eight-pointed star-shaped pod is used for flavouring meat and poultry dishes in Malaysia, Singapore, Indonesia, China and Vietnam.

22. Turmeric
This yellow coloured rhizome is related to ginger and used in many dishes in India. It is also added to Thai curries. The fresh root has an aromatic and spicy fragrance, which can be lost by drying. Turmeric is available fresh or powdered. In a recipe, 1 Tbsp chopped turmeric is equivalent to $1/4$ tsp powdered turmeric.

VEGETABLES

23. Bamboo shoots
These are the young shoots of the bamboo. Fresh bamboo shoots must be boiled for at least 1 hour to soften before they can be used. After boiling, soak them in water until required. Boiled and ready-to-use bamboo shoots are available in packets or canned from Chinese grocery stores and some supermarkets.

24. Bean sprouts
In Asia, bean sprouts are grown from either mung beans (green beans) or soy beans, while in the west they are always grown from mung beans. If the sprouts are intended to be eaten raw, they should be mung bean sprouts. Soy bean sprouts have to be cooked for 10 minutes before they can be eaten.

25. Bilimbi
This small fruit, locally known as *belimbing asam* or *belimbing buluh*, is light green or yellow in colour and resembles a tiny cucumber. It has a sour taste. Fresh bilimbi is added to dishes

such as *sambal* and curries to tenderise the meat and to give a tangy flavour. This versatile fruit can be pickled or preserved with salt and then dried and used as a substitute for tamarind (*asam*).

26. Bittergourd
This wrinkled, cucumber-like vegetable is eaten while still unripe. With bitter tasting flesh which improves when cooked, the bittergourd features in Southeast Asian dishes such as cooked salads and stir-fries. It is also made into a tart pickle and is popular in India. According to Asian kitchen wisdom, the more grooves on the bittergourd, the more bitter it will be.

27. Brinjal
This vegetable comes in two varieties – egg-shaped and long. They are either white or deep purple. The purple variety has a thicker skin, but there is no difference in flavour.

28. Cabbage
Cabbage is related to broccoli, cauliflower, kohlrabi and Brussels sprouts. Choose heads which are heavy with crisp, shiny outer leaves. Eat raw in salads. Cook only for a minimum time in a covered saucepan and drain very well.

29. Carrot
Choose bright orange, shiny specimens; avoid those with soft spots or cracks or those, which are limp. In spring, look for baby carrots with their green tops intact. Serve cooked or raw in salads.

30. Chinese mustard, preserved
This is the most commonly used preserved vegetable in Chinese cooking. This is Chinese mustard or leaf mustard that has been preserved in vinegar (*kiam chye*) and can keep indefinitely. It is used in stir-fries and soups.

31. Cucumber
Although cucumbers are usually thought of as essential for salads and with

crudités, it is also surprisingly good when braised and served as a vegetable, especially with fish and seafood dishes. Look for glossy, crisp, bright green vegetables.

32. Flowering cabbage
Flowering cabbage (*choy sum*) has green leaves, pale green stems and small yellow flowers. This vegetable can be steamed, stir-fried or blanched and used in noodle dishes, soup, etc.

33. French beans
This name encompasses a range of green beans, including the snap bean and the bobby bean. They are mostly fat and fleshy and when fresh, should be firm so that they break in half with a satisfying snapping sound.

34. Jackfruit
The jackfruit tree, native to India's Western Ghats, bears the world's largest fruit. The fruit is eaten both young and ripe. Green, with thick, sharp pines, the starchy young

jackfruit is usually cooked as a vegetable. It is a staple source of starch in many Asian and South Pacific countries, where it is fried, roasted or boiled. When ripe, it is eaten as a fruit or used in some Asian desserts.

35. Jicama
Originating from America, jicama (*bangkuang* or yam bean), locally referred to as 'Chinese turnip', are now cultivated in most countries in Asia. It has one root and is sweet, juicy and crunchy. It is an important ingredient in spring rolls or *poh pia*.

36. Lady's finger
Also called okra, this vegetable belongs to the hibiscus family. It is particularly popular in Creole and Cajun cooking. It has a glutinous texture and is a natural thickener. Soaking for 30 minutes in vinegar, diluted with water, can minimise the viscosity.

37. Long beans
Also known as the Chinese bean, this very long, narrow, dark green variety is cooked as you would a green bean.

18

19

20

21

22

23

24

25

26

27

28

29

30

31

32

33

34

38. Papaya
Indigenous to Central America, papayas range in size from very small to very large, and are eaten both ripe and green. When ripe, the papaya has soft juicy flesh and a fairly sweet taste (similar to apricot); it makes a good dessert or breakfast fruit. The unripe fruit, which has crisp, firm, tangy flesh, can be cooked as a vegetable, made into salads or used to make preserves and pickles. The fruit is very popular in Asia, where the flowers, leaves and young stem of the papaya tree are also cooked and eaten.

39. Pineapple
Native to South America, the pineapple is really a cluster of fruits of the Ananas tree that combine to form one 'multiple fruit'. The pineapple is one of the most popular tropical fruits. Available all year round, it makes an excellent dessert fruit. It can be bought fresh or canned. The fruit is delicious eaten ripe. In Asia, semi-ripe pineapple is used in sour soups and curries.

40. Pisang raja
These uniformly-shaped bananas are long and slim. When ripe, the skin is pale yellow and has a sweet fragrance. These bananas are popularly used in *goreng pisang*, where they are coated in batter and deep-fried as a tasty snack.

41. Potato
Originated from South America, potatoes are an important source of carbohydrate. Once thought to be fattening, potatoes can be part of a calorie-controlled diet. They are low in sodium, high in potassium and an important source of complex carbohydrates and vitamins C and B-6, as well as a storehouse of minerals.

Potatoes are available year-round. Choose potatoes that are suitable for the desired method of cooking. All potatoes should be firm, well-shaped (for their type) and blemish-free. New potatoes may be missing some of their feathery skin but other types should not have any bald spots. Avoid potatoes that are wrinkled, sprouted or cracked. Store potatoes in a cool, dark, well-ventilated place for up to 2 weeks. Warm temperatures encourage sprouting and shriveling.

42. Sugarcane
This is a tall Southeast Asian grass which has stout, fibrous, jointed stalks. These juicy canes produce sap which is a source of molasses and commercial sugar. In this part of the world, sugarcane is often squeezed to extract its juice and is drunk ice cold; cut into short lengths and chewed for its juice or boiled with water chestnuts to make a traditional Chinese tea.

43. Sweet potato
This elongated tuber comes in orange, white, yellow and purple. It is commonly used to make Asian desserts and is also added to salads to replace the potato. Prepare and cook as you would potatoes.

44. Tapioca
Tapioca in its fresh form is called yucca, which is another name for the root of the cassava plant. This root is also known as manioc or mandioca. When raw, it has a bland and sticky quality and is used in cooking the way you would a potato. It can be boiled, mashed or fried.

45. Tomato
Native to South America, dozens of tomato varieties are available today — ranging widely in size, shape and colour. Among the most commonly marketed are the beefsteak tomato, globe tomato, plum tomato and the small cherry tomato.

Choose firm, well-shaped tomatoes that are noticeably fragrant and richly coloured. They should be free from blemishes, heavy for their size and give slightly to palm pressure. Ripe tomatoes should be stored at room temperature and used within a few days. They should never be refrigerated — cold temperatures make the flesh pulpy and kills the flavour. Unripe fruit can be ripened by placing it in a pierced paper bag with an apple for several days at room temperature but do not refrigerate or set in the sun.

Tomatoes are rich in vitamin C and contain amounts of vitamins A and B, potassium, iron and phosphorus.

46. Water convolvulus
A green leafy vegetable, water convolvulus (*kangkung*) can be found growing wild beside streams. Some varieties have purple stems. If unavailable, substitute with spinach or watercress.

47. White radish
Also called daikon or mooli, it looks rather like a large white carrot, hence its Chinese name which literally means 'white carrot'. With a mild flavour and an ability to soak up other flavours, it is excellent for braising or used in delicate Chinese soups. It is also pickled.

HERBS

48. Basil leaf
Asian basil, also known as sweet basil, is widely used in Thailand. Several varieties are used to flavour foods. The sweet, aromatic fragrance of *bai horapa* graces many dishes while *maenglak*, or lemon basil, is used in soups. Basil leaves are best used fresh as they do not retain their flavour when dried.

49. Chinese celery
Similar in appearance to continental parsley, this is a stronger flavoured version of the more familiar celery. The colour may vary from white to dark green. Use in soups, stir-fries and stews.

50. Chinese chives
Also known as garlic chives, Chinese chives have thick, long flat leaves like the spring onion (scallion) and a stronger flavour than the Western ones. It is used both as a herb and vegetable in Southeast Asian cooking.

51. Chinese parsley
Also known as coriander leaves or cilantro, Chinese parsley is indigenous to southern Europe. All parts of the plant can be used, even the roots, which are an essential ingredient in Thai cooking. This herb is used to flavour and garnish dishes.

52. Curry leaves
Sprigs of small, shiny pointed leaves with a distinctive fragrance, curry leaves are used most frequently in south India , Sri Lanka, Malaysia and Singapore and Fiji. Fresh curry leaves are normally sautéed with onions while making curry. Dried curry leaves, which are probably easier to find in Western countries, are not as strongly flavoured, but they serve the purpose.

53. Kaffir lime leaves
These are the leaves from the kaffir lime plant. The lime is a small dark green citrus fruit with a thick, wrinkled and bumpy rind. Its leaves are easily recognised by its two distinct sections. The leaves are available fresh or dried, and are used in soups, curries and stir-fries.

54. Lemon grass
Lemon grass, a long lemon-scented grass, is popular for flavouring curries and soups in Malaysia and Singapore, Indonesia, Thailand and other Southeast Asian countries. Only the pale lower portion of the stem, with the tough outer layers peeled away, is used for cooking. If lemon grass is not available, two or three strips of thinly peeled lemon zest can be used as a substitute.

55. Mint leaves
There are over 30 species of mint, the two most popular and widely available being peppermint and spearmint. Peppermint is the more pungent of the two. It has bright green leaves, purple-tinged stems and a peppery flavour. Spearmint leaves are gray-green or true green and have a milder flavour and fragrance. Mint grows wild throughout the world and is cultivated in Europe, the United States and Asia. It's most plentiful during summer months but many markets carry it year-round.

Choose leaves that are evenly coloured with no sign of wilting. Store a bunch of mint, stems down, in a glass of water with a plastic bag over the leaves. Refrigerate in this manner for up to a week, changing the water every 2 days. Mint is available fresh, dried, as an extract and in the form of oil of spearmint or oil of peppermint, both highly concentrated flavourings.

56. Polygonum leaves
These narrow, pointed leaves are also known as Vietnamese mint and *laksa* leaves. They are used for garnishing and flavouring curries. The leaves are either crushed or sliced and used in curries or *laksa*. The leaves are also added to fish dishes to camouflage the fishy smell.

57. Screwpine leaves
Commonly known as *pandan* leaf, the long narrow leaf is used in Singapore, Malaysia, Indonesia and Thailand in savoury dishes and desserts.

The leaves, with their delicate flavour, are as essential to Asian cooking as the vanilla essence is to Western cooking. When pounded and strained to extract the juice, the leaves lend flavour and colour to Asian sweets and desserts. They can also be used to wrap marinated meat and other food to add flavour.

58. Spring onions
Spring onions, known as scallions in the United States, have long thin leaves with sometimes a white bulb at the base. Both the white and green portions are chopped and used for garnishing.

59. Torch ginger flower
This bud of the wild ginger flower has a delicate aroma. For cooking purposes, the bud is picked while the petals are still tightly folded. Its intriguing fragrance lends a refreshing aroma to curries and fish dishes. The bud may be eaten raw, where it is finely sliced and added to vegetable salads such as *kerabu* or *rojak*. The full blossom is added to soups and gravies to impart its unique flavour.

60. Turmeric leaf
The leaves of the turmeric plant are very fragrant and used extensively in curries. It is usually shredded to impart a stronger flavour.

FLAVOURING

61, 62. Coconut (whole & grated)
Coconut is indispensable in Malaysian, Singaporean, Indonesian and Thai kitchens. Coconut milk is not the water found in the middle of the coconut; rather it is the liquid extracted from the grated flesh of the coconut. The first extraction is the richest and is called the No.1 milk. Water is then added to the already used coconut flesh and squeezed again to extract a slightly weaker milk referred to as the No.2 milk.

Roasted grated coconut is often added to enrich certain dishes. This is obtained by roasting fresh grated coconut, stirring constantly in a dry pan over low heat until it turns golden brown.

Coconut milk and grated coconut can be found in supermarkets, fresh, canned or powdered, which can then be reconstituted with the addition of water.

63. Kaffir lime
(*See 51. Kaffir lime leaves.*)

64. Kalamansi lime
The juice of this small, round, green citrus fruit is very sour. It adds a tangy flavour to dishes and drinks. It is also referred to as 'local lime'.

65. Lime
This small, lemon-shaped citrus fruit has a thin green skin and a juicy, pale green pulp. Limes grow in tropical and subtropical climes such as Mexico, California, Florida and the Caribbean.

Look for brightly coloured, smooth-skinned limes that are heavy for their size. Small brown areas on the skin won't affect flavour or succulence but a hard or shriveled skin will. Refrigerate uncut limes in a plastic bag for up to 10 days. Cut limes can be stored in the same way up to 5 days. The versatile lime has a multitude of uses, from a sprightly addition to mixed drinks to a marinade for raw fish dishes to the famous desserts.

52

53

54

55

56

57

58

59

60

61

62

63

64

65

OTHER INGREDIENTS ● ● ● ● ●

66. Almond
Almond is the kernel of the fruit of the almond tree, grown extensively in California, the Mediterranean, Australia and South Africa. There are two main types — sweet and bitter. The flavour of sweet almonds is delicate and slightly sweet. They are readily available in markets and, unless otherwise indicated, are the variety used in recipes. The more strongly flavoured bitter almonds contain traces of lethal prussic acid when raw.

Almonds are available blanched or not, whole, sliced, chopped, candied, smoked, in paste form and in many flavours. Toasting almonds before using in recipes intensifies their flavour and adds crunch.

67. Anchovy, dried
These are salted and sun-dried anchovies. They are available in wet markets and Chinese grocery stores.
To store them, remove the head and intestines, rinse quickly and dry thoroughly before storing. Fry them in deep fat when they are dry and they make delicious, crisp snacks that go well with drinks.

68. Black prawn paste
This prawn paste is not to be confused with the dried shrimp paste, or *belacan*, which is more commonly used in Asian cooking. Neither can this be used as a substitute for *belacan*. Black prawn paste (*hay ko* or *petis*) is a black, molasses-like paste made from shrimp, sugar, salt, flour and water. It is most famously used in Penang *laksa*. It is often an acquired taste and has a smoky, earthy pungent flavour.

69. Candlenut
This hard, waxy and beige nut has a slightly bitter taste. Small quantities are pounded or blended into a paste and used as a natural thickener. It also adds a nutty texture and flavour to curry dishes. To prevent it from becoming rancid, store candlenuts in an airtight container in the refrigerator.

70. *Char siew*
This is lean roasted pork where the surface of the roast has been coloured red. It is often sold alongside roast duck.

71. Chicken stock cube
Chicken stock is obtained by boiling and simmering of chicken bones and carcass for several hours. The stock is strained and refrigerated then its solidified fat that rises on the surface is removed to get a virtually fat-free stock. This stock is then frozen in ice cube trays for future use. Chicken stock is used to give flavours to the dishes.

Ready-made chicken stock cubes can be bought at the supermarkets.

72. Chinese cruellers
These are long fritters of dough which has been deep fried in pairs, so they stick together. In Taiwan, it is eaten for breakfast with soy bean milk. In Singapore and Malaysia, it is often chopped and added to porridge or to *tau suan*, a hot dessert made of green beans. Its name is literally translated to 'oil fried devils', and refers to the fate of a husband-and-wife pair in ancient China who betrayed a well-loved hero.

73. Chinese mushrooms, dried
These are dried shiitake mushrooms and vary in size and price, depending on quality. Soak them in hot water before use. Resume soaking liquid to add to the dish while cooking, or into stocks to lend a richer flavour.

74. Cloud ear fungus
This white fungus should be soaked in water to soften before use. When soaked, it bloats into a large, crunchy sheet. With no taste of its own, it offers a crunchy texture and is commonly used in Chinese stir-fries or desserts.

75. Crisp-fried shallots
Crisp-fried shallots are shallots that have been sliced fine and deep-fried in hot cooking oil until golden brown. They are used for flavouring and garnishing. To make them at home, peel the shallots and finely slice them crosswise. Deep-fry in hot oil over low heat, stirring briskly all the while. Turn off the heat as soon as they turn a pale brown. Remove and drain on absorbent paper until cool. Store in an airtight container.

76. Dried prawns
These are sun-dried, salted, steamed prawns. Soak them in water for about 20 minutes to remove excess salt before using. Dried prawns are ground, chopped or left whole and fried to flavour dishes.

77. Dried sour fruit slices
Dried sour fruit (*asam gelugur*) slices is a tangerine-like fruit that is sliced thinly and dried in the sun. Light brown when fresh, it turns darker as it ages. Like tamarind (*asam*), it is used to give acidity to cooked food.

Dried sour fruit slices are usually available from Chinese grocery stores. If not available, substitute with tamarind pulp.

78. Fish maw
Fish maw is the air bladder of the fish. Its main function is to receive and expel huge qualities of water and/or oxygen so that fish can ascend and descend in the water. This makes the bladder very strong and elastic. Dried fish maw is mostly used in the preparation of thick soup. It is effective in relieving coughs and beneficial for the general health.

79. Golden needles
These are unopened flower buds of orange and yellow day lillies. At certain times of year, you may find fresh lily buds in Asian produce markets, with bright golden petals tightly folded above an emerald green calyx. They are delicious stir-fried with minced pork and flavoured with garlic, black pepper and fish sauce. Lily buds are known as 'golden needles' because of their original colour, though once dried, they fade to a pale brown. Popular with Buddhists and other vegetarians, they add a distinctive, earthy flavour to a dish.

The long, slender dried buds of the day lily (*kim chiam*) are sold in packets and will keep well if stored airtight. Look for buds pale in colour and still flexible, not dark brown and brittle, which indicates they are old. Store

in a jar with a tight-fitting lid, away from the light. Before adding to a dish, soak in warm water for 20–30 minutes. Trim soaked buds of hard stem, then either tie each in a knot, shred by tearing, or cut across in halves.

80. Indonesian black nut
Although native to Brazil, this black, hard-shelled nut known locally as *buah keluak,* is grown extensively in Indonesia. The black oily kernel has a slightly bitter taste. A good nut is heavy, does not rattle when shaken and does not produce a hollow sound when tapped lightly.

81. Lime paste
A white substance obtained by burning and grinding cockle shells until fine. It is usually eaten with betel leaves. It is available in some speciality baking stores.

82. Orange peel, dried
Often added to soups and casseroles, it gives a distinct and pleasant orange flavour. The best peel comes from large, brightly coloured fruit. The peel is threaded into twine and dried in the sun for a week. It is often sold in packets and can be bought from most Chinese grocery stores or herbalists. Soak for 20 minutes before use. Keeps indefinitely if stored in an airtight container.

83. Palm sugar
Also known as jaggery, palm sugar is made from the sap of the palm tree. Fresh palm sap is boiled into a concentrated heavy palm syrup. This syrup is poured into bamboo section to solidify into cylindrical shapes. Palm

66

67

68

69

70

71

72

73

74

75

76

77

78

79

80

81

82

sugar, also known as *gula Melaka* or *gula kabung* in Malaysia and *gula Jawa* or *aren* in Indonesia, is used for both savoury dishes and sweets.

84. Peanuts
The nuts have a papery brown skin and are contained in a thin, netted, tan-coloured pod. Peanuts are also called groundnuts or earth nuts because, after flowering, the plant bends down to the earth and buries its pods in the ground. Peanuts are sold unshelled and shelled. The former should have clean, unbroken shells and should not rattle when shaken. Shelled peanuts, often available in vacuum-sealed jars or cans, are usually roasted and sometimes salted. Refrigerate unshelled peanuts tightly wrapped for up to 6 months.

85. *Poh pia* skin
These are large, tissue-thin skins of rice flour dough which are used for making spring rolls. They are sold in packets of 25 or 50, and if frozen, should be thoroughly thawed before using. They are becoming widely available in supermarkets,

though some specialty artisans still make them fresh and continue to be in great demand among *poh pia* aficionados. Keep unused wrappers in plastic wrap or covered with a damp cloth until ready to use; once they have dried out, they break easily and become impossible to fold.

86. Preserved Tientsin cabbage
These brownish-green pieces of the stem of the Chinese cabbage that has been preserved in brine (*tung chye*). It has a savoury, mildly salty flavour and a firm, crisp texture. Sold in jars, it can be bought from Oriental markets. Rinse thoroughly before use.

87. Processed cuttlefish
The cuttlefish, which resembles a rather large squid, has 10 appendages and can reach up to 6.5 metres in length. It can be prepared like its less tender relatives, the squid and octopus, but must still be tenderized before cooking in order not to be exceedingly chewy. Cuttlefish are most popular in Japan, India and many Mediterranean countries. Dried cuttlefish is

available in some Asian markets. It should be reconstituted before cooking. To reconstitute, soak in warm water for several hours, then simmer in clean water.

88. Red beans
Also known as adzuki or aduki beans, red beans are usually cooked during celebrations in China and Japan because red is considered an auspicious and lucky colour. The beans are usually boiled with sugar and mashed to make fillings for sweet cakes or sweet soups.

89. Salted fish, Penang
Dried and salted fish are a Malaysian speciality. Highly flavourful, it is used in small amounts in curries and sambals. It is also added to stir-fries to lift an otherwise bland dish.

90. Salted radish
This is finely diced radish preserved in spices and salt to get golden-brown morsels that are crisp and eaten as a relish (*chai poh*). There is also another type known in Chinese as *tai tou choy*. The latter is made from whole radish cut into slices lengthwise and with all the

leaves intact, salted and dried.

91. Sesame seeds
Native to India, sesame seeds have a strong, pleasant, nutty flavour and are frequently used in breads, salads and to make oil. They are available in black and white varieties.

92. Shrimp paste
Dried shrimp paste is made from small shrimps, which have been dried in the sun before being pounded into a paste. This strong smelling condiment is widely used in Malay and Nyonya cooking. It is pounded and blended with other spices and seasonings to make a spice mix which is the base for *sambal* dishes, curries and spicy gravies. Dried shrimp paste can be bought fresh whole or as pre-roasted granules.

93. Sugared winter melon
This is winter melon (*tung kwa*) crystallised in sugar. Often sold in the dried foods section of a Chinese grocery or supermarket, it is used in various Chinese desserts (*tong sol*) and home made barley water.

94. Tamarind pulp
The tamarind fruit or *asam*, is commonly used in Southeast Asian cooking. The long pods contain pulp-covered seeds, which are usually dried and sold. This pulp is soaked in water for about 10 minutes and strained of any fibres and seeds. The sour juice is used, and adds fragrance and flavour to dishes.

95. Wheat
Wheat is the world's largest cereal-grass crop. Its status as a staple is second only to rice. Wheat contains a relatively high amount of gluten, the protein that provides the elasticity necessary for excellent breadmaking. Though there are over 30,000 varieties, the three major types are hard wheat, soft wheat and durum wheat.

96. Yellow bean paste
Popular in Nyonya cooking, this light brown paste is made of preserved soy beans, and lends an earthy, salty flavour to dishes. A variation of this paste incorporates chilli and is sold as spicy bean paste.

 83
 84
 85
 86
 87
 88
 89
 90
 91
 92
 93
 94
 95
 96

SOY BEAN PRODUCTS

NOADLES ● ● ● ● ○

WRAPPER

97. Bean curd (firm and soft)

Firm bean curd (*taukwa*) is pressed and quite heavy. It is the firmest bean curd of all and very versatile.

Soft bean curd (*taufu*) is available in slabs from the wet market or in rectangular containers and tubes from the supermarket. It has the texture of custard. Handle carefully to prevent breaking it. There are several varieties of bean curd including silken bean curd and cotton bean curd which is slightly firmer, but not as firm as *taukwa*. It is also available combined with egg, and sold as 'egg bean curd'. These are often cylindrical in shape and sport a distinctive yellow shade.

98. Bean curd puffs

Known as *taupok*, these are deep-fried bean curd puffs, which are either round or square in shape. They are light, with a golden brown exterior and a soft, somewhat 'honeycomb' interior. Whether it is stuffed with fish or meat, or is eaten as it is, it has an easy to chew texture, which gives it a very distinctive taste. Like all bean curd, it absorbs other flavours well.

99, 100. Bean curd skin and sticks

Dried bean curd skin can be found in stick and strips (*foo chok*) or sheets (*foo pei*). This comes from the thin, yellow layer that forms on the surface of soy bean milk before it coagulates. *Foo chok* is commonly used in desserts. *Foo pei* comes in sheets about 60-cm wide. They are sold folded like plastic sheets and are available at stores selling bean curd, Chinese grocery stores and supermarkets. Do not refrigerate them.

101. Sweet bean curd strips (*tim chok*)

These are small, seasoned, brown rectangular pieces of dried bean curd known as *tim chok*. These are used mainly in vegetarian cooking.

102. Cellophane noodles

The vermicelli-like noodles are made from mung bean flour. They are also called glass noodles or bean starch noodles. They should be soaked in water before being added to boiling soups or stir-fried vegetables. Cellophane noodles (*tang hoon*) are used in Japanese, Thai Burmese, Vietnamese, Chinese, Malaysian, Philippine and Indonesian cooking.

103. Coarse rice vermicelli, fresh

Made from rice flour, these *laksa* noodles are as thick as spaghetti. Dried rice vermicelli can be used as a substitute if fresh noodles are not available.

104. Fine wheat vermicelli

These Filipino off-white dried wheat noodles (*mee suah*) are very slender. They can be deep-fried to make a crunchy nest or boiled for 2–3 minutes to make a salad or be added directly to soup.

105. Rice noodles

Made from rice flour, these flat, opaque noodles (*kway teow*) are about 1-cm ($1/2$-in) wide. They are available fresh or dried and can be boiled or fried. Dried noodles should be soaked for up to 30 minutes to soften.

106. Rice vermicelli

Rice vermicelli (*bee hoon*) is made from rice flour. It can be fried or cooked in a soup. The dried variety needs to be soaked first in cold or hot water to soften, then drained, before cooking.

107. Yellow egg noodles

These large, yellow noodles are made of wheat and are either round (often called Hokkien noodles) or slightly flattened (*mee pok*). They should be rinsed and drained thoroughly before being fried. Like all fresh noodles, they should not be kept for more than a day before using, otherwise they tend to become heavy.

108. Banana leaf

Used in almost every Asian country, the banana leaf is often shaped into cones, square containers, neat rectangular packages to be used as wrappers, or to take the place of a plate. When used as a plate, the mid-rib of the leaf is retained. As a wrapper, the mid-rib is removed. Before shaping it, blanch the banana leaf in boiling water briefly to render it pliable.

97

98

99

100

101

102

103

104

105

106

107

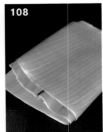

108

INDEX TO THE GLOSSARY OF INGREDIENTS